BARRINGTON
CLUB DAY

A Cotswold village celebrations re-lived

JIM LAZENBY

First Published in 2003

Published by Jim Lazenby 2003

© Jim Lazenby

ISBN 0-9546634-0-3

Acknowledgements

My warm and sincere thanks to those people not already mentioned in my introduction.

The Wingfield family of Barrington Park for allowing me to include so much of their lives.

My sister, Doreen Hunt for checking and correcting the first draft.

Mrs Muriel Preston, Mrs Millie Cambray, Mr Keith Herbert, Mr Alan Sollis in lending some of their photographs and their help in naming individuals.

My friend Mr David Shayler who printed this book and assisted in its composition. His favourite charity will benefit.

Mrs Mary Tudge, who, on Mr Shayler's enthusiastic recommendation, ably prepared this book for publication.

Mr David Viner, Chairman of the Cirencester Historical Society, for his supportive and valuable advice.

Mr Harold Sambell, long time owner of Butts Studios who undertook to search his archives, find and print several negatives hitherto unseen.

And certainly to my wife Mavis for her welcome patience and encouragement.

Assuredly I shall have made some errors, possibly even indiscretions. My memory serves me well enough but is not infallible.

Should you feel prompted to enlighten me and perhaps help putting names to individuals not identified in the photos, I shall be delighted.
Jim Lazenby, Little Barrington, Burford, Oxon OX18 4TE will find me.
No e-mails!

INTRODUCTION

I was born in the village of Great Barrington, Glos in 1926. Except for a short sojourn in Windrush, fully three quarters of a mile away, I have always lived in the parish of Great Barrington. This surprisingly includes some half of Little Barrington as well as The Inn for All Seasons, formerly The Barrington New Inn.

My enthusiasm for attempting to write a short story about my childhood era has been prompted by several reasons.

On reading a short article I had written for Saga relating to the Soul family, Libby Davies, one of many people who have, perhaps, been bored by my many tales of "the old days" suggested I should commit them to paper. After much heavy persuasion I submitted to her an untidy draft, which I had penned a while previously. She undertook to get it onto her computer, a machine about which I plead absolute ignorance. Without this one and few more "boots up the rear end", (her words) it would probably never have seen daylight.

I had for some time realised that very little of the ordinary lives, or indeed of the characters, of previous generations had been recorded.

There is little continuity of tenure left in these wonderful Cotswold villages. The sons and grandsons of our previous generations who had expected to follow their ancestors, living in the same houses and working within the village limits have all but disappeared.

Their houses, one might almost say their birthright, once peopled with large friendly interrelated families now house an interesting mix of urbanites. They come from all points of the compass, some even from faraway shores, some returning to their roots and only identifiable by their different accents.

Where one house now stands, invariably occupied by only two people, two and sometimes three separate cottages were within these same walls; large families in each. Six children in a virtually one up and one down dwelling was usual enough.

To redress my remarks, I happily concede that without this influx of new money many, many dilapidated, even derelict, cottages and barns would have decayed and been lost to posterity.

Quite soon, the only strong links with the past will be preserved by the sons of the old land owning dynasties.

During my childhood in the 1930's my mother caused me to paste newspaper cuttings of very local interest into my "Whopper Scrapbook". Browsing through them has caused me to appreciate and relive a second childhood. They are excellent and very full records of many village activities. Egg and spoon races, sack races, three-legged races, Sunday School outings, children's amateur dramatics, adult as well as children's fancy dress competitions, cricket matches and more. All these possible because of the large and close kindred of a village population which scarce strayed beyond its boundaries.

I now express my very sincere thanks to Mr. Peter Davison, editor of The Wilts and Glos Standard for so readily agreeing to their inclusion in this book. Much of the content must have been as a consequence of the reports from my grandfather and mother who, for many years, acted as local reporters for this same newspaper!

Just in case you should puzzle why I was dressed as "DORA – Shuts one eye today" in the Coronation fancy dress photo! It was to depict the Defence of the Realm Act whose dictates were allowed some relaxation that day. Notably, all day drinking instead of the then rigid public house hours 10am–2pm, 6pm–10pm.

Advisedly or not, I have included a few words of local dialect. I hope they don't detract from the contents. Wireless and then television, mobility of our various peoples, even the concentration of schooling into large assemblies has caused a rapid loss of real local language – I find this a great pity and when I'm with any of the few remaining "natives", David Cambray or Mervyn Garratt for instance, we delight ourselves by reverting to it. Many an "old tale" can only be appreciated this way.

Having no children of my own to treasure the accomplishments of my family, particularly my mother and grandfather, I now feel some relief that I can commit these memories to your care.

There are some, who on learning that this part fun, part serious amble through the past has been restricted to such a short period, have been a little disappointed. To them I say that I have already started on my next venture. The intriguing and colourful, village wartime period in which I was quite actively involved!

Jim Lazenby, Sister Doreen and Mother Ruby

Ruby Lazenby Née Barrett

Jim, Doreen and 'Peter', 1936

NOTE: The full funeral reports at the rear of this book have, after much thought, been included. The many local names and family representatives could well bestir faded memories. I feel that descendants wherever now settled, will be intrigued by them. They, like much I've written, can only be of very local interest.   JAMES E. LAZENBY

CHAPTER ONE

The atmosphere in the classroom was charged with excitement, sharp young ears were straining to identify any slight sound from the outside world and behind the headmaster's back the big boys from the mixed class were rising from their desks to peek out of the windows. It was the Friday afternoon before Whit weekend, the day when it would all begin.

Those huge windows, bigger than any others in the whole village, except for those in the Big House, were maddeningly, tantalisingly and deliberately placed a few inches above the young scholars' eye level. The Victorians who had designed and built the solid edifice in local Cotswold ashlar limestone would brook no distraction from the teaching of the three R's. The tops of a couple of apple trees and the roof ridge of the girls outside lavatories were the only objects to ponder on. The apples would be soft and mushy, not worth eating, but then, when they were ready, so would many more around the village be there for the "apple scragging" season when twilight raids would add to their flavour. The girls toilets also used by the infants, were seats over buckets, which were emptied at the back of the smelly building. To further exasperate his charges, the headmaster, standing, seemed to spend more time than usual looking out of the windows.

The familiar view from the village, standing on its south facing slope of the Cotswold hills, ranged down across meadows and fields, hedges and trees to the River Windrush, its busy flour mill and on up over the twin village to the great wooded ridge, which carried the main A40 coaching road from London to Fishguard. The magnificent new Village Hall stood to the left of the playing field where once a stately row of beech and elm trees held sway, but more of this later.

The spring sunshine streamed through the windows, lighting up the familiar contents of the room. The wooden desks, now ink-stained since slates were put aside, had been individualised by the village offspring, the wall map, the easel and blackboard. It burnished the gold lettering of the names on the Honours List above the fireplace, the ones who had passed the exams for Northleach Grammar School. Most had gone on to their further education, but others, whose parents had been unable to afford the twin burdens of school uniform, although subsidised and extended school years, had stayed on to leave for work when they were fourteen years old. Most were from large families and two extra years "earning no keep" were just not possible to sustain.

Jim supposed that one day his name would be there too; he would soon be taking the entrance examination. He'd found school easy, but then he should have, his grandfather James Barrett had come there as headmaster in 1883, soon after leaving Culham College, where, Jim was told, the students, mostly of theology, were prepared for the clergy and for schoolmastership. Despite the top honours, evidenced by the many prizes of beautiful bound leather books on theology that had been awarded to him, he lacked the private means then necessary to "take a living" in the Church. When in 1925 he retired, Mr. Arthur Gibbs, whose qualifications though probably admirable, had never satisfied him, had replaced him. Therefore, despite many battles with the school attendance officer, he'd managed to keep Jim at home and give him a good grounding and a head start over the rest.

For a school with so many pupils – up to 110 – the silence was tangible, broken only by the scratch of pens, the clink of inkwells and the occasional petulant cry from the door leading to the infants' classroom, where Miss Olive Herbert, in fear of the head, endeavoured to keep the necessary order.

MR GIBBS CLASS, BARRINGTON C. OF E. SCHOOL 1937

Back Row Bert Phipps, Keith Herbert, Henry Dadge, Sidney Tidmarsh, Muriel Smith, Cyril Cole, Joyce Keylock, Cyril Tidmarsh, Pat Busson, Kathleen Parker
Second Row (Standing) Cyril Phipps, Jack Stocks, Ron Keylock, Frank Workman, Bobby Browning, Doreen Lazenby
Girls (Seated) Margaret Cambray, Peggy Sollis, Freda Houlton, Frances Sollis, Hester Clements
Front Row Tom Jennings, John Clements, Jack Dadge, Jack Sollis, Eric Workman, Jim Lazenby

Barrington
C. of E. School

The sun played on the brass top rail of the fireguard, or rather on those parts of it, which could be seen. The fire, burning warmly, was all but hidden by several white handkerchiefs hung over it. Mr. Gibbs had one of his interminable colds and found it very handy to dry them out there as they became ever more sodden. He turned to the mantlepiece to shake out another cigarette from that big round yellow tin of Gold Flake, so far removed from the paltry paper packets of five Woodbines bought by most of the parents, lit it from a match – such a waste when he could so easily have used a spill from the fire – waved it gracefully to extinguish it and spun round to face the class. This sudden volte face was far too quick for the lad who'd been taking another hopeful look outside.

"Sit down Herbert, the next boy I catch looking out of the window will come out here for three of the best". Watty Herbert (cack-handed like Jim) sat down, looking a little more than relieved that it wasn't his turn to be made an example of. Both had been lucky enough, when beginning school, to have escaped the previous practise of correcting left handed writers and forcing them to use their right hand. This often had disastrous effects on a child.

"Sir, can I be excused?" Sidney Mills seemed to have come up with the perfect solution.

"No, you'll wait 'til the end of the lesson!"

Perhaps sensing a real urgency, "Oh go on then, but be quick."

The boys latrine lurked along a short path, screened by a forbidding yew hedge and boasted one cubicle, little used, because of the fear of having the corrugated iron door burst open by jeering lads, and a space where one was confronted by more six foot high vertical sheets of corrugated iron embedded in a concrete plinth which boasted a shallow gully to drain off the piddle. These iron sheets over the years, acquired infinite and disgusting shades, ranging from the original black at the top, through greys, browns and bright orange, which served to indicate how high the user could pee.

The highest points reached were usually as a result of a competition. Other than the lone boy, excused from class, practising on his own, break-time saw a small row of boys exhibiting their skills, helped not only by their age and superior development, but by the urgency of their need. An extra foot in height up the rusty target could be achieved by pinching the end of the most insignificant penis, to release the pent up pressure in a glorious spout of steaming amber liquid. Genuine acclaim was reserved for the lad who could go over the top and he'd walk away strutting like a Leghorn cockerel.

No one washed their hands afterwards; indeed, where or how could they? There was virtually no running water in the village, no taps, no bathroom and no flush loos. The Big House, the tenanted farmhouses, Jim's home – the Old Vicarage, but few others were served by piped water from the estate. Everyone else had to carry it from the three pumps strategically sited along the only street. Two bucketfuls fetched at a time didn't go far in a cottage household. It was augmented from the rainwater butts outside every back door. Water for shaving, cut-throat style, water for washing and even for bathing in the tin baths occasionally. Never mind the shoals of silver fish, the decomposed remains of luckless mice and sundry other unfortunate wild life that had been trapped and sunk to the bottom.

"No, you can't come in, Dad's having his spring bath!"

All the lavatories were in stone-built and stone-tiled outhouses. Earth closets – a big vault dug out, served by a wooden seat with a shaped hole in it and screened by yew trees.

Jim's home lavatory had the advantage of a double vault. He assumed that as it had once been a Vicarage, two separate lavvies were built, one for the family and one for the servants; but, as in death, all things are equal, so, by means of a large duct between the two vaults did the effluent achieve that level state. Only one was now in use, lurking behind the inevitable yew tree, apple trees and snowberry bushes. These all thrived on the regular but very infrequent emptying of this capacious system.

The emptying was achieved by a couple of bucolic village men who, fortified by a healthy consumption of homemade wine, amidst clouds of tobacco smoke, dismantled the wooden double seat, heartily applied themselves to the Herculean task of scooping out the dark brown mess which was perceptively enhanced by squares of rotting newspaper and heaping it among the grateful bushes and trees.

Peels of laughter, lewd jokes and the sound of much hawking and spitting beset that part of the garden from which Jim and his sister had been expressly excluded. No one fell in but they could scarce have smelt worse if they had. The job done, the seat reinstated, all that remained was an application of quicklime to speed the eventual rotting of the noisome mess.

The lavatory was candle lit and if the candle wasn't extinguished by wind or rain whilst negotiating the path from the house door to it's dark, smelly and eerie confines, the guttering flame, for seldom was the door shut, served to illuminate the hole in the board seat and to find the damp and yellowing squares of newspaper stacked to one side. Toilet rolls were barely known and would have been far too expensive for such a crude purpose.

The candle also afforded Jim the chance to look into and explore the vault by lowering it at arms length into the murky depths. Cobwebs and spiders, beetles and millipedes abounded and a ledge where the front board overhung the floor was discovered. One day using this knowledge he, to the astonishment of a small group of friends, lowered himself through the hole, small toe-caps finding the ledge and folded arms supporting him on the lavvy seat grinned triumphantly at his incredulous peers. This particular feat, on being discovered by his mother, created an awful stink in every sense of the word.

The headmaster, sensing diversion, then walked briskly over to a door, which led, by way of a corridor to a third classroom, where the children of intermediate age were taught. He jerked it open to discover a small boy standing in "The Space"; erect, but cringing, ashen faced, blinking in the sunlight. "The Space" had been created by an accident of design. It was a black hole, formed by the inclusion of a second solid door, some thirty inches from the first, which acted both as a draught excluder and sound barrier. It provided a perfect punishment cell for the child unfortunate enough to incur the displeasure of Miss Augusta Susan Woods.

She, assistant head, whose task for many years was to teach and discipline that section of the school before they moved up to the top class, was much feared and respected. A strong, angular, indestructible, bespectacled spinster with eyes in the back of her head. She moved so quietly around a subdued class that the pain inflicted when she flicked the back of an unsuspecting ear was exaggerated by the shock of her presence.

"Garratt, what have you been doing?" The unfortunate lad sent to stand in "The Space" for pulling a girl's hair, having waited in fear, listened in dread to every footstep in the adjoining classroom, and hoped against hope that the afternoon would end without a sortie by the headmaster into this end of the school, was suitably admonished and returned to class.

"Sir, can I fetch another bucket of coal?"

Jack Sollis tried the next clever ploy. The coal was kept through the back door of the old prison, adjacent to the school. This village lock-up had long ceased its original function. When it was built it marked the intersection of three county boundaries, Gloucestershire, Oxfordshire and an isolated part of Berkshire. The village policeman lived in the house opposite, now number thirteen.

Jim could hardly foresee that one day, on his marriage, Colonel Wingfield would offer him the choice of four village cottages. He chose number thirteen – always the optimist! It had the massive advantage of running water and a stone sink. There was, and presumably still is, an iron-ringed flagstone in the living room floor. He refrained from lifting it so never discovered whether it was a well, or, fancifully, an underground passage to the prison.

"Don't be a silly ass, sit still," was Mr. Gibbs' reply.

"They be coming!"

The word spread rapidly around the classroom. Some of the boys, country ears alert to the slightest sound, able to hear a rabbit thump as it dived into its burrow, half way across a field, had detected the jingle of brass, the rhythm of hoof beats or the crunch of iron-bound wheels. The hands of the large wall clock stood at ten to four. Forty more minutes before school would end.

There was no suppressing the class now. Even the girls were infected with the mounting tension. More unrest amongst the boys.

"Come out the front Jennings."

The head gamekeeper's son was the first to suffer. Arm out straight, hand out flat, three stinging blows and back to his desk. Moist-eyed, smiling bravely, honour intact. Good old Tommy, Jim's best pal. Raised in a hard school, son of a firm and unbending father, Alfred Jennings, late of the Coldstream Guards, fearful of no man, servant only to the squire. Standing tall and erect, clad in heavy thornproof tweed, polished leather boots and leggings, battered trilby hat, jay's feather tucked into hatband. His thumbs hitched into the old service belt, Coldstream Guard buckle thrust forward, proclaiming, "Finest regiment in the British Army", he was no man to trifle or argue with. His conviction was absolute and none had cause to question it.

All gamekeepers have and need to have a cruel streak in their nature to enable them to pursue their calling. Alfred was in the front rank when that doubtful virtue was awarded. Pity the poor kennel lad found without a yard-broom in hand, shirking from slopping out the kennels with disinfectant or spoiling a skin when removing it from some hapless vermin. Mole, stoat and even rabbit skins were scraped, stretched and tacked onto the wall of a sunlit, wooden outbuilding to dry.

He lived in the head gamekeeper's house down by the river and kept the garden, kennels and stables immaculate. At the bottom of the garden was an eel trap, a pond fed by the spring which supplied the household water by means of a hand-pump in the outhouse, and a channel from the main river course. The water was held back by a wall riddled with holes which prevented the eels from escaping. Long disused, it was perfect for another venture.

Tommy and Jim spent wondrous days fishing down the river, which was full of chub and dace. They went armed with a bucket and brought their catch back to the much silted-up pool. Some of the poor chub were so big that they could scarce move without their dorsal fin cutting the surface. Winter flooding seemed to return them back to the main river.

No Land Rover to patrol, guard and nurture the game on his dominion. Simply a long and unflagging stride uphill and downhill over meadows, heavy, ploughed land, through marshy bogs and thorny undergrowth. A pony and trap to fetch the feed and bring in the day's bag after the shoot. His guns were racked above the living room mantelpiece; a sixteen bore for small vermin, twelve-bores and one heavy weapon for culling the deer in the Deer Park. These he butchered and hung in the game larder in the big house outbuildings equipped with pulleys, chains and hooks. Favoured friends received choice cuts of venison.

He could drink at The Fox, play cards, losing with bad grace, shoot anything that interfered with his pheasants and partridges, and, to preserve the trout, used an uncanny judgement of reaction and deflection to shoot the predatory pike.

He would quickly despatch any ailing dog or cat brought to him.

"Tie him to that tree and I'll see to it."

When his own faithful retriever bitch was past her best, he calmly instructed her to sit and used the same gun she'd served so well to "put the old girl out of her misery!"

Poor Tommy had feared for his life when he burnt the stable down whilst experimenting with matches. His mother, terrified, hid him behind the settee in the front room until dad's temper had cooled a little. The leather belt with buckle was a fearsome object. Learning from this, Jim made a similar retreat when Alfred Jennings came looking for him. He'd been walking a field with Bobby Browning, another friend, a tenant farmer's son, he with a small Diana airgun and Bobby with a four ten shotgun. Suddenly a cock pheasant erupted, screeching, from a pile of brushwood and flew directly away. No one, but no one except the shooting party shoots a pheasant. Murder and poaching were on a par, with the accent on poaching.

"Have a go you" shouted Bob.

Up with the airgun, down with the cock, only one possible point of entry. A practical demonstration of being "shot up the arse". Cruelly, the keepers other son saw its demise, picked up the evidence, took it to father, who after failing to find Jim at home, left his parents instructions for "a strict dressing down".

The hands of the clock, "creeping like snail", had registered a welcome time.

"Alright, collect the books and tidy your desks." School over at last. "Off you go and behave yourselves this weekend. Back on Tuesday". An urgent, jostling rush to the door, caps and satchels snatched from the cloakroom pegs and a mad scramble to be first into Back Lane.

Mr H. J. Barrett and assistant teachers, Miss A. Woods on the right

Lane opposite school – Number 13 is on the right, small house on left now gone

CHAPTER TWO

They were there.

A long line of gypsy caravans and wagons had drawn onto the grass verge. Some shaped like boxes, most with hoop-shaped tops and others revealing tantalising shapes under threadbare canvas. Some gaily painted and others of sombre hue, the whole teeming with life. Swarthy, dark-complexioned, black haired men in black trilby hats, collarless white shirts and black waistcoats. Women with long, lank, dark hair, some hanging loose, others in a high bun, wearing fine black shawls and long sweeping skirts; urchin children, some scarce clothed and others in long trousers. Strange hungry looking dogs all legs and tails, skulked, trembling amongst the equipment now being pushed under the vans.

Horses everywhere, some still in the shafts, others still haltered to the rear of the caravans and many pegged out to browse the grassy banks. Even a pony and a couple of foals. Working horses, but so different to the farmers shires, with their plaited manes and tails and their huge fetlocks. These, small chestnut brown ones with long, flowing manes and switching, stinging tails. Dusty and sweat-stained, quiet and content.

The fair had arrived. Every part of it strange and alien to the wondering group of rustic children watching it from a safe and circumspect distance, the boys in short trousers and hob-nailed boots and the girls in calf-length skirts.

"There's the swings you, and there's the roundabouts. Look at they kids, they ent got no shoes on" and so the chatter progressed.

"See that old bugger over there , ee's the one as 'ouldn't give I a coconut as I knocked off last year, says as I should have stood back on the mans' line."

"That old girl's the one as read our mum's fortune last year, said as er ad to cross er 'and with silver first."

"See all they clothes pegs, they'll be round a selling they tomorrow."

Long rows of hand-whittled and split willow pegs, bonded by thin strips of tin tacked in place, were ready for the morrow, when the women would wheedle and cajole the ladies of the village to part with a few coppers. Also small bunches of "lucky heather".

"Cross my hand with silver missus, or you'll be having a year's bad luck".

Fires were already burning on the verges, smoke was wafting lazily from thin smokestacks on some of the caravans and large black pots were beginning to simmer on hastily contrived hearths. Youngsters were dispatched to go and fetch buckets of water from the village pump. The rabbits, hares, hedge-hogs and more covertly the pheasants, caught by the Lurcher dogs, were going into the cauldrons.

For Jim, time for tea. A quick and wary trot past the new arrivals, round the corner, over the wall, across a small field, avoiding several large black sows, over the open iron-rail fence and onto the front lawn. Not that the sows held any fear for Jim, he had once been caught and chided for trying to coax milk from the swollen dugs of a reclining sow.

Tea with sister Doreen, Mother and Grandfather. Without Grandfather Barrett, none of this excitement would be happening. Monday would be Whit-Monday, but here in this isolated valley, it was Barrington Club Day. The annual day of celebration of "The Barrington and District Working Mens' Benefit Society".

There was no National Health Scheme or Social Security to care for the family whose man was taken ill or injured at work. They could only survive by going "on the parish" which tendered a pittance and by the help of hard-pressed neighbours. In extreme circumstances they were forced to go to the workhouses, those gaunt and austere buildings, still to be recognised in most small country towns, now converted into hospitals, old peoples' homes and, as in Witney, into factories.

Mr. Barrett, whilst being headmaster of a school of some one hundred and ten pupils, the village postmaster, organist and choirmaster had recognised the plight of some of the locals. He then founded this Benefit Society, later copied by a similar one in Cirencester, which paid out a sickness benefit to its members. A weekly contribution of sixpence would produce a useful ten shillings a week. It was regulated by a committee, which met regularly at his house. These were men like Edward Hayward, the builder from Little Barrington and Charles Griffin the miller. People well placed to recognise and assess the validity of the claims and the immediate needs of the members. The Club was wound up, with a touch of bad humour and agitation in 1950, some ten years after the death of its founder, superseded by the Bevan report, with its subsequent health and family advantages, and impoverished by the decline of most of its assets which had been patriotically invested in $2^{1}/2\%$ War Loan Stock during the First World War.

Tea over and away again to see the gypsies. There weren't so many schoolboys there now. Those from the villages of Little Barrington and Windrush, those from the outlying farms and keepers' cottages, all trudged off home, many of them five year olds and faced with a daily walk of up to three miles each way. No wonder their mothers couldn't keep them in shoes, but their safety was never in question.

The scene was much the same, though muted, animals and people resting after the long haul and welcome sustenance. Where did they come from, and, like the house martins, how did they manage to find their way back and arrive on the right day? Where did they go for the rest of the year? Did they all stay together or did they arrive from different horizons?

There was some tentative chat between the two groups, but attitudes, dialects and accent preserved a gulf between them. After a while Gerrard Lobb fished out his mouth organ and red-faced, sweating profusely, played songs new and old.

Gerrard's father, Daniel, was head cowman on the estate with a stentorian voice and an awesome shout. He'd stand by the dairy buildings and call the cows in from fields away. Sleek doe-eyed Guernseys, full udders swinging from side to side as Daisy, Rose, Buttercup and the others lurched upfield to line the milking stalls, eat their ration of food, ruminate and enjoy the relief of their bursting teats.

Investigation of this preserve was fraught with danger for a small boy. The golden rule was "watch their tails". If the tail starts to rise, get clear or be covered in a copious spray of liquid, sweet-smelling cow muck ejected effortlessly and horizontally. Stay away from Blossom, she kicks violently and keep a safe distance from the robust, perspiring man, white-capped head into a cow's flank, perched on a three-legged stool, teasing out gallons of creamy, white milk into his shining pail. The ping-ping of the jets of liquid striking the bottom of the pail changes in note to a viscous ssh-ssh as it fills to the top. Get too close and with an adroit flip from the milker you would get an eye or mouthful. A bowl of hot bread and milk might well be good for the convalescing infant, but straight from the cow could turn the stomach over.

Daniel, like many of his compatriots, had come up from the West Country during the hungry twenties. Farmers and farm labourers alike had settled up on the cold, brashy Cotswold hills.Tremaines, Trevellyans and Trelaws were now local names.

Gerrard's mouth organ droned on; a remarkable feat by a boy who found schooling a difficult task, he could hear a tune and play it straight back, songs and snatches of tunes from the Great War, others marking various troubles and times.

Grandfather's Boer War produced the Mafeking Surrender song:

> On Mafeking night, on Mafeking night
> We'll all get tight on Mafeking night
> We'll all be merry, sticking pins in the Kruger's belly
> On Mafeking night, on Mafeking night.

Galipoli:
Oh the moon shines bright on Charlie Chaplin
His boots are cracking
From want of blacking
And his little baggy trousers they want mending
Before we send him
to the Dardanelles

Edward VIII's Abdication
Hark the Herald Angels sing
Mrs. Simpson stole our King

The Abyssinian War
Will you come to Abyssinia, will you come?
Bring your own ammunition and a gun
Mussolini will be there, shooting bullets in the air
Will you come to Abyssinia, will you come?

"Well, I be off home you, wur bist thee off to?"
"I be off home too, got to help dad feed the pigs."
Pigs were a precious part of the economy. Every cottage had its own sty and most had at least two pigs to fatten. Kitchen waste, potatoes, apples and pig food were boiled up and carried down to the pungent pigsty. Hours and hours were passed by the cottagers; elbows on sty doors, considering and appraising the relative qualities of their own, as well as their neighbours' pigs. Nothing more satisfying than leaning over to scratch the back of a fine animal that would one day feed the household. The gardens were lush from the pig muck, cabbages like footballs and spuds like ostrich eggs, what a marvellous by-product.

Home now for Jim too, he had to go to bed early. Most unfair, why should he have to lie there listening to more fortunate kids catcalling and hallooing around the village war memorial, which was just outside his window? Strong voices in the making.

Not for the countryman, a quiet word of acknowledgement when passing the occasional acquaintance on a city street, but a loud hail from any distance, long or short, across the road or the other end of a field. Countrymen nationwide can always be distinguished from the town-dwellers, they talk from deep down in their chests, so at variance from the poor sounds produced by the Brummies, Cockneys and Scousers of this world. Just listen to the men of Dorset, Norfolk and Gloucestershire to name but a few. The dialect may be different but the intonations are the same.

The eagerly awaited excitements of the weekend to come must have caused Jim to awaken early. He was suddenly conscious of a flurry of hoof-beats, it was 5.30 a.m. and he looked out of the window to witness the morning rush of carthorses. They were always turned out at night into a field at the bottom of the lane, which passed the house. At this ridiculously early hour, Tom Herbert the carter for the farm opposite, would go down, storm lantern in hand, open the gate and free this bunch of ten or a dozen great shires, who then rushed pell-mell up the lane, across the metalled road to find their stables in the farm. Here they munched their oats and bran and were readied for a long day's work in harness. On dark mornings the only warning of their presence in the unlikely event that a vehicle was using the road, was the flash of sparks as their hooves kicked the granite road chippings. The other carters and ploughmen would be there at 7 a.m.

This new surface to the local roads which had until recently been "white", or stone and mud was costing the boys' mothers dearly. The steel shod heels of their hob-nailed boots could, with a hard dragging kick, light up the evening gloom with quite amazing sparks. It was only a couple of weeks ago that the local council had carried out a second 'tar spraying'. This had involved a steamroller and a team of men, all tar-spotted, but with one, Arthur Busson from Windrush, actually spraying the liquid tar. This had been brought in great chunks, put into a coal fire heated cauldron on wheels and hand-pumped through a tube to the operators' nozzle. He had to heavily grease his skin and cover himself as best he could in tar encrusted clothing. The heat and smell must have been stifling. When he pushed up his goggles the better to see what he was doing, the white of his eye circles contrasted with everything else about him.

Others wheeled barrows from which they showered the freshly tarred road surface with chippings and the steamroller shunted back and forth to finish the job.

Nevertheless an uneven surface ensued and caused many problems when whipping tops, or even chasing hoops down the street. Tops were perhaps the best game of all. The small wooden blue and red banded kind with a round-headed nail in the bottom to spin on. The whips could easily be made by pinching whipcord from wall hung pictures. A deft whipper could chase it, spinning down the street and the only danger was that on occasion the energetically whipped cord would lift the top and propel it, sling shot fashion, through a cottage window.

The best hoops were blacksmith made from lengths of solid round iron, whilst old bicycle spokeless rims would suffice.

Soon the local cockerels began to crow. One next door, two across at the farm, other mournful notes carried in the still, clear air all the way from the mill and even from the far village.

Then a terrible squealing from hard by, a heart rending, spine chilling sound, to cause the scalp to crawl, the nerves to jangle and the stomach to turn. The screams and squeals of the death throes of an old friend, gradually subsiding and finally quiet. It wasn't difficult to picture the scene at the pigsty down the lane. Caleb Stratford, the village pig-sticker, razor sharp knife in hand supporting the dying animal while its life-blood gushed into a bath from a terrible wound in its throat. Then the straw and brushwood fire to burn off the hair from the carcass and finally the expert butchering. The request, "a bucket for his guts Mum", the careful extraction of that most prized possession, the bladder, probably to be used, after being dried and blown up, by the local Morris Men.

The meticulous use of every scrap; tail, trotters, head and brain, chitterlings and blood made the pig the perfect choice animal where economy was paramount. Various cuts, large and small, to take round to relatives and neighbours who would reciprocate when their own pig came in, allowing fresh pork to be enjoyed often enough. Great hams and sides of bacon to be cured and salted, the sides destined to be hung on big strong hooks in the smoky living room, treasured and admired above the companion pictures of "Monarch of the Glen," "Bubbles" and our mum's sampler.

Chitterlings, intestines, to be turned inside out, cleaned, washed and made into faggots. Brawn to be cooked and savoured, and mouth-watering fries of liver and onions. A long and hard, but wonderfully rewarding labour of love and necessity. For those unfortunate enough to lose their prize pig through disease or other calamity, a "Pig Club" was formed.

Fat bacon, spuds and cabbage, the mainstay of the community. Many the lump of fat bacon, bread and a bottle of cold tea, carried in raffia bag, for sustenance during the long plodding hours following the plough in the far-flung fields. Men clothed against the harsh winter weather in ancient ex-army overcoats, thick, coarse trousers tied at the knee with string, hob-nailed boots and leggings contrived from old army gaiters, Gopsil Brown sacks or even the tops of worn out wellington boots.

These same men were the survivors that had been lucky enough to come home after that long and bitter 1st World War. They were very reticent to recount their experiences to the next generation, but it was inevitable that Jim wondered at them. Too many memories of the hellholes of the Flanders trenches, too many thoughts of their local friends and colleagues perishing in such a futile and barbaric manner. Indeed, one family, the Souls had lost five out of six sons. Jim's mother regularly had the dreadful task of delivering the War Office telegrams, "We have to inform you", to their mother. Her response, on opening the door to see her there, had haunted her all her life. "Not another one, my dear?"

Others, like Frank Faulkner, had been shipped out to serve on that romantically named Northwest Frontier in north-west India. The idea that these same quiet, stolid and gentle farm men had travelled to and fought in such a near mythical and far-distant country was truly difficult to believe.

No wonder that November 11th, Armistice Day had such sombre and tearful connotations. The church service, when two minutes silence was observed after which the names of the fallen were reverently recalled echoed only part of the nations' grief. In hamlet, village, town and metropolis the whole populace became silent, caps, trilbies and bowlers doffed for those dreadful two minutes. Workers and bosses, children and mothers, cars and transport ceased their days movements and, ram-rod still, the country mourned its dead.

The residue of the unfortunates, the wounded, were evident everywhere. Blind men, men with broken spirits and so many like Roland Preston and Harry Smith with wooden legs, still cheerful in adversity and thankful for their lives after receiving a "Blighty One", a wound serious enough to precipitate their homecoming and an end to their sacrifices and tribulations.

"At the going down of the sun and in the morning we will remember them."

Those absent, cheerful and innocent young men, who had volunteered for and been called to join the ranks of their shire regiments; the Gloucesters, the Yeomanry and the Oxford and Bucks Light Infantry. Hardly a family in the land untouched by this tribute, which will continue for generations to come.

Showing Frank Faulkners house and the "Hollies" Mr Gibbs house

CHAPTER THREE

Time at last for Jim to get out of bed. Father's just off to work and he must keep out of his way. "Little children should be seen but not heard", was the general rule, but his father required they should also remain unseen. Scotts Porridge Oats for breakfast, chop some firewood and rush out into a bright spring morning. Down the lane, past the now silent pigsty, smelling and seeing the evidence of the early morning slaughter and, suffused with excitement, past the now busy, strung out encampment to join the group of lads loitering at the far end. They were always abroad earlier than him, their fathers having risen to start work. The working week being 7 a.m. to 6 p.m. and including Saturday morning.

The gate into the "playing field" was open and the fair people were moving in the last pieces of their wares and equipment. With practised ease, these wagons, full of boards, spars and canvas were converted into a motley collection of swings, stalls and roundabouts, gaily painted and seductively inviting.

By one caravan a big cauldron was bubbling away next to a small, painted but chipped, trestle table, its sugary contents had now reached a dark brown, semi-fluid consistency. The gypsy ladled out a mound of the contents to cool a little on the table and started making rock. Bare armed, in pearl buttoned waistcoat, he stood briefly, spat thickly on his hands, rubbed his palms together, seized the lump of brown sugar, stretched it as using a chest expander and threw the centre of that great glistening mass up and over a conveniently placed hook screwed to the side of the caravan. Another pull, place both ends together in one hand, unhook the other end, throw the centre of the ribbon back over the hook, pull and repeat time and time again. The sugary band gradually changed colour as it aerated from dark to lighter brown and after another generous hawking of phlegm to cool the palms, it was thrown and thrown again until the time when it acquired a creamy white colour. More brown sugar was then put on the trestle, stretched into similar lengths and mixed with the white to form a wide band of colours. This was chopped crosswise to form the finished delicacy, home-made rock, brittle as marble and nearly as hard.

The whole process seemed so unhygienic that Jim always determined never to eat any, but for sure, when an uninformed relative bought him some, that resolution would soon be blown.

The swings stood ready, the roundabout, revolving on its central pole, with its centre space for that little pony to trot round and round, lugging its load of exultant infants, was nearly ready. The coconut shy, the roll-a-penny stall with its dextrous, poker-faced minder and the shooting booth were all fixed.

The shooting booth was the most popular with the lads. Two shelves, just above head height, on which stood, well spaced, packets of ten Players, ten Woodbines and boxes of England Glory matches. Big airguns, much bigger than the boys had at home, rested on the board in front of the booth. These were adapted to fire corks, hopefully to knock the prizes off the shelves, knocking them flat didn't count, they must go off the shelf.

Having seen the completion of all these preparations, the lads then made their way to the top of the village, settled themselves on the low wall around the war memorial and watched the world go by.

Cars, lorries and motor cycles were still rare enough to generate their own interest. George Hall, the blacksmith in his Model B Ford seemed always on the move. Cloth-capped, car interior strewn with nails, tools, horseshoes and leather apron, he was, fortified by frequent tots of rum at The Fox,

The New Inn and other local hostelries, kept very busy. He also doubled up as the local taxi. Passengers and car survived somehow. The old crash gearbox suffered most and at times when the double de-clutch operation failed to synchronise and select he could be heard shouting at it amidst the crash of gears, "If you wun't go in that un, get in there, you bugger, you be all in there some-where".

Harry Barnes, the estate foreman, bumbled by in JB 9, his little Austin 7. Mr. Barnes was also the local cycle repairer with a quite comprehensive, dark little workshop attached to his house. A quiet, gentle and practical man who could turn his hand to a thousand other repairs needed in those days of make do and mend. To buy anything new was both difficult and irresponsible!

Three buses served the village, Basil Howse's bus from Aldsworth to Cirencester on a Thursday and Cheltenham on Saturday, and "The Red Bus" to Burford, also on a Thursday. "The Red Bus" ran from Stow-on-the-Wold, via the local villages to Witney. To underline the remoteness of the villages it is worth recording that, to promote the service, posters were displayed asking the question, "Been to Burford?" Burford was three miles away. This became a catch-phrase and greeting for certain villagers who had indeed made this pilgrimage. "Bin to Burford, you?"

There was the sound of a big engine labouring up the hill. "Here's another Tom Morris a coming", said one of the lads. "It's a Bedford", "No it ent, it's a Dodge" argued another. A big dumpy Dodge truck hove into view, protesting at its load of aggregate, hauling it still further, another four miles uphill, to add its small contribution to the completion of Little Rissington Aerodrome. There on the cab door was the chequer board motif and the legend, "Tom Morris, You move, We move. Gloucester."

The aerodrome, nearing completion, destined to become the R.A.F. 8 MU and 6SFTS, was fast pitching the locality into the twentieth century. Thousands of loads of sand and gravel were creating mayhem on the small local roads and the teeming wildlife. "Yers one a coming down fast." With some disappointment, amidst a screech of brakes and tyres, the young audience watched the drivers avoid each other on that blind bend. Those trucks and drivers had to keep rolling to deliver their payloads.

Meanwhile there were uncomfortable stories about the on site contractors, who were basically paid by the number of lorries working there. Tales of broken down trucks being regularly towed from one area to another so as to be included in the head count.

"What sort of aeroplanes will they have up there then, you?"

"I reckon they will have some of them Tiger Moths and some of those De Havilland planes they has at Witney for training".

"No", said George, whose father was working up there, "They be going to have some big uns with only one wing and two engines, they call 'em Avro Ansons."

The thought of the skies being filled with aeroplanes was a great novelty. Jim recalled seeing air-ships. The R 100 had flown low down the valley from west to east when he was very young, and not so long ago when he was coming back from church with his grandfather one dark evening, a great shape, the German Hindenberg, had flown right across the village with a big spotlight shining down, which lit up the war memorial. The wise men of the village concluded that the Jerries were spying and that rumour persisted until the next Great War.

Jim was also reminded of his first recitation:

> "Aeroplane up so high, will you take me to the sky?
> I can't get there by bus or plane
> So will you take me aeroplane?"

Britain, scarce realised by the locals, was preparing for war. Aerodromes, built to the same pattern were emerging all around Brize Norton, South Cerney and Heyford, to name but a few. The main impact of all this activity was yet to be felt.

"Jim a telegram for Rissington".

His mother had hurried from the house with the usual buff envelope.

"Oh no, not today", he thought, but he knew that he must go. Telegram delivery provided him with a handy supplement to his pocket money and the sixpence he would get for cycling three miles each way would be useful at the fair. Twopence for Great Barrington and fourpence for Little Barrington. Living in a Post Office gave distinct advantages. The telephone was never the fearful instrument, which worried generations to come. Knowing the recipients of foreign post helped stamp collecting and also, by careful removal, faintly marked stamps could be transferred to his own letters to be well cancelled when date-stamping the outgoing mail.

This was a very satisfying chore, accomplished by thumping the hand-held cancelling stamp first onto an inkpad and then onto the stamps and letters. A halfpenny for a postcard and a penny to send a letter.

Anyhow, it was all downhill coming back from Rissington. Thankfully it was an infrequent chore, there being a Post Office there anyway, which only closed for the usual half day or because of illness.

The ride to Rissington caused a late lunch, and then it was off to the fair proper. This time he got into the field by the top gate, passing the two massive walnut trees.

He hoped that this year would bring a good crop, walnuts are a particular delicacy. This year he would try to catch them at the right time for pickling, not with shells already set and woody. They must be big enough but still soft; last year had been a catastrophe. Later they would be gathered as soon as the huds had started to split and they dropped to the ground. Impatient as always, the boys would slink, hopefully unnoticed, to throw sticks, a yard long, at the branches and rain walnuts to the ground. The stain from the huds and the churned up mud under the trees and the slop of the cowpats into which most of them fell, was quite ineradicable by anything less than a pumice stone and gave the game away to parents and schoolmaster alike.

Later in the year the gates to the great Deer Park at the big house would be thrown open for "Walnutting Day".

This was another day in the village calendar when by permission of the squire, the children invaded those secret and sacred acres of trees and grassland. Buckets, barrows and old prams were filled with walnuts and taken home to keep through to Christmas. These nuts, full of fresh, white kernels when first picked up, invariably fell to the ravages of mice and rats, or mildewed away into a grey mass unless properly dried.

A few people had started to wander round the fair, the plaintive call of encouragement, "come on son, it un on the top, threepence a go", was being directed at men and boys alike. This afternoon was only a warming up period, everyone knew it and most were reluctant to spend their few shillings yet.

Fred Clifford took the initiative and like a flock of sheep, the others followed. A big, strong, quick-tempered youth, he made short work of dislodging a coconut and stood back for the rest to follow. The stall-holder replaced the nut, deftly scooping out some of the sawdust from the top of the holder, making it nearly impossible for the next hit to unseat it.

"Come on lads, up to this mark here for the littl'un."

But to no avail. These country boys, practised at "buzzing stwuns" at rabbits and birds, some say "strong in the arm but weak in the yed" could hit them all right, even cracking them, but failing miserably to dislodge them. "Hit em on the top", he shouted again and making great play of lifting a nut by its whiskered top, the showman replaced a few flakes of sawdust to make it look easy.

Tiring of this, they made off to the swings. Strong, eager young arms clasping the ropes and pulling with might and main. Big heavy wooden swings gathering momentum, higher and higher, boys now standing up and pulling even harder, the centre of gravity shifting, the whole framework juddering and jumping to free itself from the restraining iron pegs. An exhilarating sensation killed abruptly by the shout, "Slow down you young sods or I'll stop you now".

The creak of the protesting ropes and excessive movement soon subsided.

"We a got to 'ave our monies worth, ent us?" was the reasoned argument. Soon, too soon, came the clonk, clonk of the brake, a board fixed at one end below the arc of the swing and lifted powerfully at the other to make contact with, brake and stop the swing.

Now over to the shooting booth. To boys raised on shotguns and air guns this must be a steal. "Tuppence a go". With Players Navy Cut at sixpence for ten and Wills Woodbine at fourpence, it seemed reasonable enough. The air guns were cocked and loaded with corks and the serious business began.

Take aim, sight dead on that packet of Players, only a few feet away, pop, nothing. That's impossible, thought Jim. Next shot, same result, but a sharp eye had followed the cork which went six inches top right. Third shot, lay off, six inches bottom left, pull trigger and hey presto! Collect the John Players. Hold back, don't seem too eager, wait 'til Cyril Cole has stopped using that particular gun, go back in, grab it, and using the same tactics, finish up with more cigarettes and a box of England's' Glory matches. Baleful looks from the sour-faced proprietor, who puts that gun away, mean beating a strategic retreat.

The last time that he'd actually owned a packet of cigarettes had been on a school trip to Swindon to see how a factory was run (see report page 77). Having already been to the Morris car factory at Cowley, Oxford and been conducted through the huge workshops, watching men assemble the cars. It was, Jim supposed, logical enough to visit the Wills tobacco factory in Swindon.

It was also an encouragement afforded to the many thousands of school children, who would have done the same trip, to start smoking and to smoke Wills brands in particular. They saw the whole process from tobacco leaf to neatly packaged cigarettes, and as they left the last section where the cartons were being filled, they were all presented with small, gift-wrapped, packets of "fags". (See School Outing reports page 77.)

By now, a knot of village women had assembled by the top wall. Large, long-skirted and pinafored, most with bonnets or shawls, they regard the scene through curious, though uncommitted eyes.

There's Mary Newman, spinster, with black hair done up in a bun and a luxuriant black beard. No need to pay at a side-stall to see a "Bearded Lady". Mrs. Kitchen, a hard-working washer-woman, still wearing the same flat cap that she wears all the time, even when she comes to Jim's home every Monday morning to do the weekly wash. Then the fire under the "copper" has been lit early and most of the black smoke is belching out of the drainpipe chimney.

The air is thick and moist with the steam from the copper, its bubbling contents, wet laundry in Persil, the tin tub with the finer garments in Lux flakes and the final rinsing in Reckitts blue, before all is pegged out on the washing-line, create a never to be forgotten aroma.

Miss Mary Newman

Mr & Mrs Percy Pratley and daughter Ivy
He was head woodman at Gt Barrington

Mrs. Daniel Lobb. A big lady, with heavy, dark tresses.

Mrs. Percy Pratley, with her daughter, Ivy, in a wheelchair. A stalwart lady who besides a family of four boys, has to look after her husband, care for an invalid daughter and take on casual jobs to augment the family income. With wonderful good grace, she will skin and prepare the odd rabbit or hare that Jim's mother might take to her, keeping the skins to sell on to Skinner Stevens from Sherborne, when he makes his regular visits to the village.

Her husband, Percy, the head forester was born at Leafield, which he always referred to it by its old name of Field Town, under the shadows of the once great Wychwood forest. He was a stickler for punctuality. There he would be, by the park entrance, waiting, pocket-watch in hand, for his men, intolerant of late risers, but straight and fair. They were always home on time, carrying the best shoulder sticks. Shoulder sticks kept fires burning. A good, five-foot long, thick bough, carried home comfortably across one shoulder every day was the norm for a needy countryman.

The same Deer Park entrance, by the war memorial, served the old coachmans' house. The coachman, Mr. Papworth, was a jocund, impish man with twinkling blue eyes, whose duties had now fallen foul of the advance of progress. His coaches were gathering dust down in the Home Farm buildings, chickens were laying eggs in them and a head chauffeur had usurped his position. For a man with a fund of redundant expertise and intimate tales of his previous masters, who included the Earl of Sandwich and the Duke of Buccleuh, before his long service for his present squire, life must seem to have dealt him a cruel blow.

Mrs Papworth

Mr George Papworth
Head Coachman

A visit to his house elicited a pleading enjoin-der by his wife to be quiet because "Dad's listening to the wireless". The long aerial strung on poles across the garden led into the front room and the "crystal set". Sitting by, large earphones on his head, he could be seen patiently probing with a "cat's whisker" to find the spot which would relay any audible sound. Once found, woe betide his timid wife if she disturbed the contraption while dusting.

Time now to retire to the Bowsen, a stonebuilt, thatched cattle byre standing at the top of the field. This, despite its pungent, dung-filled floor now littered with fresh straw, would serve as the beer tent. Indeed a couple of untapped firkins of Garnes' Burford bitter, spile pegs bubbling, had already been racked so that the sediment could settle. While some of the older boys now felt free to have a furtive drag on their newly acquired Woodbines, others played with matches. A good game was to wrap the red tip in silver paper, lay it on the table, silver tip overlapping the edge and heat it with another match. The result was that it shot backwards with a crack like a cap pistol. Not surprisingly, matches were taboo since Tom burnt the stable down.

Eventually teatime called Jim and he went off along the lane, passing four huge elm trees growing just over the wall. Three boys were leaning over the wall watching something at the base of one with some interest." Come and see Sammy, he's tossing off". This meant nothing to him but he joined them. Now four boys in a row, peeping over the wall at Sammy, who, settled into a natural cleft in a big tree and screened by another one was, surprisingly, jerking, pale-faced and sweaty at his puny penis, now erect but hardly remarkable. Not comprehending the reason for this apparently aimless pastime and getting quickly bored with the whole scene, Jim left them for the more important pleasure of eating. Nevertheless as he went, he was reminded of the stranger who, similarly ensconced in a tree in the same field had been causing some puzzlement and interest among the innocent semi-circle of young boys and girls watching him practice the same art.

After tea the fair hotted up, the whole village going down for a look and to spend the odd shilling, but bedtime was early and so for Jim the day finished.

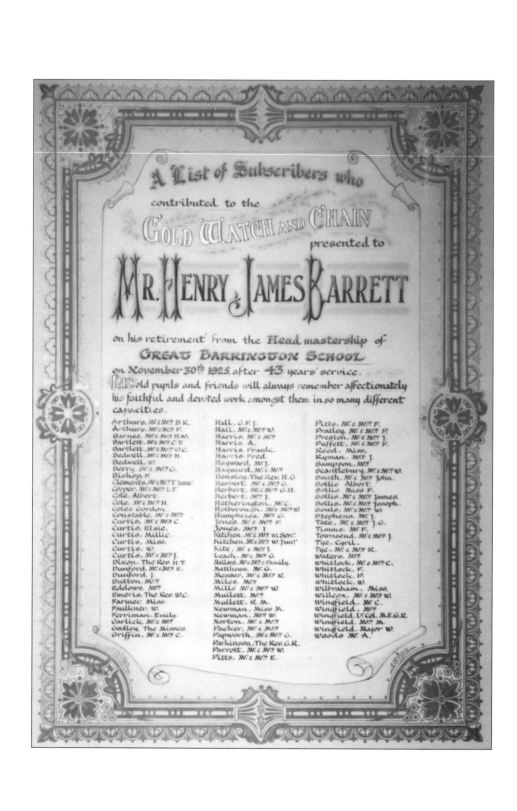

CHAPTER FOUR

Sunday morning broke clear and fine again. For Jim, Sunday meant Church. He rose quite late so as to have breakfast when his grandfather returned from the 8 a.m. Holy Communion. No food or drink until that service was over; Church on Sunday was obligatory. Inevitably as his grandfather was organist and choirmaster it meant going to every service other than Communion. Initially as choirboy and, later, when the treble voice had cracked, he would blow the organ. The choirboys and girls were marked in a register and annually were paid a penny for each attendance. The organ blower got twopence.

Indeed, grandfather, Henry James Barrett, lovingly performed these duties for 57 years. When he died after a very short illness in 1940, Mrs. Kathy Hall, the blacksmith's daughter-in-law, quickly and competently took them over until failed health forced her to give up in the year 2000. At that time each parish had its own vicar and organist, but because the present one now serves five parishes and organists are few and far between, she had to extend her talents to cover the other village churches. These two dedicated people had served a grand total of 117 years. Surely a record! Report of Mr Barrett's funeral in Appendix.

Sunday too, was a day of rest, so no fairground for anyone that day. No business for the gypsies either.

Breakfast over, there was time to play in the garden with his sister Doreen until the call to get ready for church. What had been a prized Victorian croquet set, a game which had declined into oblivion, now served more as a cross between games of cricket and golf. The fine wooden handles of the mallets were getting broken and split and the heavy wooden balls were chipped and scuffed from contact with gravel paths and stone walls skirting the lawn.

Whit Sunday, a special day in the church calendar. Eleven o'clock matins. Grandfather in a dark grey suit, waistcoat sporting the gold Albert chain of his solid gold Benson half hunter watch. This was presented to him with an illuminated framed scroll displaying the names of nearly every family in the village, who had subscribed for it on his retirement as headmaster. Trilby hat and walking stick completed the picture as he left early enough to sort out the music and play voluntaries as people filled the church. (See page 22 for photographs and report of Presentation in Appendix.)

Time now for the young choirboy and choirgirl to go. From the house a short walk to church, downhill under more towering elms, seeming even bigger because the road was several feet below the height of the walled field where they stood, a couple of yards back.

Under them posed several of those same sleek Guernsey cows, chewing their cud and slowly, gracefully, swivelling their heads as they watched the people pass, their elevated position adding to their sense of dignity. The fresh green foliage of the trees seemed far removed from those ankle deep piles of dry, gold, brown autumn leaves, which after the first crisp frosts would fall gently to cover the road. It would then be fun again to drag and kick ones feet through them propelling cascades of vary coloured hues ahead.

In 1940, long before Dutch Elm disease so cruelly decimated our elms, these magnificent trees were to be disfigured by another quirk of nature. It was a terribly hard winter and the area awoke one morning to a world of shimmering ice. There had been a fall, not of snow but of supercooled rain. It froze immediately onto everything it touched. Every blade of grass, every twig, every surface was covered in thick, shining, clear ice.

The telephone lines were as thick as ships hawsers, the weight of the ice stretching them so that they dropped in deep curves to the ground. The huge telegraph poles along the A40, carrying some forty wires each, now superseded by underground cables, snapped like matchsticks, causing absolute chaos by severing inter-city communications during the depths of a war-time winter. The eerie quiet was continually shattered by agonisingly loud reports as the tons of ice took their toll on nature itself.

By walking over a crackling field, where every blade of grass had assumed the perfection of a glass blower's dream. Jim was to stand, surrounded by beech and elm trees and watch in awe as the grossly overladen branches, some dipped to the ground, broke off with a terrifying shriek and plunged from on high, carrying others with them in a deafening, sparkling, incredible mass. The bird population was also decimated. Their claws were frozen to their perches and their feathers welded together.

The church path was overhung by mature beech trees. When it rained the drops collected in huge spots. These would fall heavily and at funerals they could splash onto the bare headed and sombre followers of the funeral bier, adding more misery to their grief. The bier, an iron and wooden trolley on miniature cart wheels, squeaked, groaned and rattled as it bore its burden to its final resting place. The churchyard was full. The centuries old tombstones bore witness to human frailty. Big headstones, with still decipherable carvings, dates and names, some monolithic structures and others whose limestone carved characters had all but gone. It had therefore been necessary to consecrate a cemetery away from the church. So it was along the church path, flanked by high walls, the park drive behind one and the vast kitchen gardens of the big house behind the other, across the village road and up a grassy path over Locks Orchard that the cortege made its way.

Autumn would see this path strewn with tough, brown leaves and beechnuts. The nuts, small and triangular in shape yielded little light kernels whose taste seemed to bear no resemblance to that new innovation, the hard sugar coated Beechnut chewing gum.

The church bells were ringing their usual and insistent tune. "The leaves are red, the nuts are brown" and then, timed to perfection, they stopped and the ting tang began as they arrived at the church door. There was a heavy and pervading perfume in the air. The church was full of fresh flowers. White flowers for Whit Sunday. White lilies at the altar, flowers at the lecterns, organ trestle and all along the window ledges. A good-sized congregation had already gathered and grandfather was playing a voluntary as they joined the other children in the choir stalls. Young boys in the front, Jim's age group next, the men tenors behind and old men with bass voices in the back row. The ladies and girls were in separate pews.

Jim became aware how everything seemed to shine. "Church cleaning", the feverish annual ritual of Spring Cleaning carried out in every home also included the church. A veritable army of determined ladies, mopped, polished and swept away every vestige of dirt and dust. The pews gleamed and the silver suspended lights shone with brilliance. The children, armed with sticks and wicker carpet beaters, carried all the hassocks and carpet runners outside to lay into them with gusto amidst clouds of liberated dust. The normally quiet and solemn churchyard for once echoed with shouts and laughter.

Like so many village churches this one is part of the baronial complex. The squire needing only to walk through his private door from his garden path to arrive there. The vicar, the Reverend Gerald Parkinson, was robed and ready to process up the aisle, but held back until, with an audible click, the private door at the top of the chancel opened and the squire and his family entered to assume their seats on either side of the chancel. Here in privacy they sat, surrounded by memorials and plaques proudly proclaiming the ancestors of their great dynasty. Here they could observe and appraise the attendance and the conduct of their minions and from here the squire could move easily to the lectern and read both lessons. He read them in a fairly high monotonous voice but commanded an absolute silence and stillness seldom achieved by an accomplished orator.

Whitsun hymns, No 154 "When God of old came down from heaven, in power and wrath he came" No 155 "Spirit of mercy, truth and love, Oh shed thine influence from above". Young trebles trying hard to be heard above the rest. George Berry, bass, holding on to the last note for far too long, but stopped in the end by a loud aside, "Cut un off short, George" from Caleb the pigsticker, who, as well as being verger, was blessed with a good bass voice.

George Berry

Caleb Stratford

Being verger then was a considerable task. He had to ascend the stone steps of the bell tower every day to wind the big church clock. He had to tend the coal fired furnace in the stoke hole below the tower which heated the water for the big pipes running under the aisle grating. Only a very early start could be effective. He was captain of the bell-ringers and ran a very able team. He was also the harbinger of bad news. He was the first one to be informed of a death in the community, nearly always a night-time occurrence, so that he might toll the dead first thing in the morning. To awake and hear that dreaded "Bong-Bong-Bong" was to be stricken with a terrible dread that it might be a close relative that had died.

Bumps, rattles and sighs from the rear of the organ heralded the conclusion of the sermon. That would be John Clements, the current organ-blower, pumping away at the long wooden handle to supply the air for Jim's grandfather to play the collection hymn. Up and down on the handle, anxious eye on the lead weight, which, suspended on a cord running over a small pulley wheel, before disappearing into the depths of the organ, must be maintained well within the E for empty and F for full marks etched on the plain wood. Woebetide the sleepy boy who allowed hymn or psalm to peter out in a panting, hollow sigh.

A strangely different atmosphere to this job!

Actually sitting in church, unseen, yet surrounded by solemn faced, obviously devout Christians, men in Sunday best, ladies all prim and proper in their lacey finery and their heads covered in a bewildering assortment of felt hats and best bonnets; yet able to unwrap another pellet of Beech Nut chewing gum, or add ones initials to those already carved in the wood and stonework with the penknife that, with a piece of string, was a statutory piece of every schoolboy's pocket.

Providing a screen and therefore a small corner is a prone stone effigy atop a large stone plinth. Despite the organ and the organ blower's desecration, he slumbers on through the ages. He wears his sword and scabbard on his right side. 'Tis said it's a sign of disgrace because he would not be able to draw it with his right hand. But, Jim always wondered, maybe like him, the knight was not errant, but left-handed or would he then, in the Middle Ages, have been forced to use his right hand, rather than risk being branded a man of doubtful character?

Out now into the sunlight, turn right and up the path through the graveyard. Flowers on a number of the graves which, though ancient, were still tended by the children and grandchildren bearing the same names which had been perpetuated by generations. Indeed, just about everyone in the village was related in some direct or roundabout way.

Sollis, Herbert, Cambray and Curtis families accounted for at least half the population. Jim's Grandmother's grave on the right, she'd never known her grandchildren, having died young from diphtheria, leaving two very young daughters to be raised by a widower, who never remarried or truly recovered from the experience.

Diphtheria was then a killer. She, another accomplished theologian and loved by the village, had contracted the disease, which affected and closed the throat, eventually cutting off any passage of air. Everything known was tried, including the inserting of a hollowed out wax candle to breathe through. In the jargon of those days "she sank into a crisis" and never pulled through. To help, and to avoid disturbing her, voices and sounds were hushed. Even the roads were laid deep in straw to muffle the sounds of the hooves and cartwheels. Her husband was eventually laid to rest by her side, the last interment in the churchyard.

Home now to traditional beef and Yorkshire pudding. Father sitting at the head of the table, carvers in hand, son and daughter subdued, worried flutterings from Mother and a resigned peace from Grandfather. No use trying to hurry the meal which was interrupted by crass comments.

"Look at the way that boy's holding his knife. I'm not sitting here and watching that. My father used to have a little stick by his side and he'd have flicked my wrist for less than that".

Perhaps he'd got punishment on the brain. Mr. Piggott, the headmaster had caned him, on his last day at Burford Grammar School, or maybe some of the army discipline still rankled.

He'd volunteered and served in the Army Service Corp. Already an apprentice mechanic at Leigh's in Witney, he stayed with motorcycles. His only brush with death was during the 'flu epidemic of January 1916 when nurses wrote letters, which the family still treasure, keeping his parents informed of his near demise and of his slow recovery. By 1918 and demobilisation as corporal, he'd adapted well to the army and temptations of the big city. So much so, that by practising some native cunning he somehow contrived to assemble a motorcycle for himself from boxes of spares and tools he'd forwarded to Shipton-under-Wychwood railway station. Later he was able to cultivate his chances by caring for the old BSA owned by his future father-in-law.

"Can I get down please?" "No you can't until you've finished that barley kernel pudding and until I tell you so".

He'd eat barley kernel pudding every day but Jim hated the stuff.

Mr & Mrs W. Mills
John Clements' Grandparents

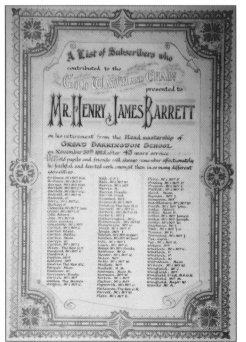

Illuminated Scroll
and Watch
referred to on page 19
(Watch is kept at
the bank!)

CHAPTER FIVE

"You can go now".

A very quick, though seemly exit to find the lads outside. Sunday afternoon was for walks. Long walks. By mutual assent, the five of them made off for Mill Lane; the Tidmarsh twins, Sydney and Cyril, John Clements, George Brown and Jim.

The high hedges were resplendent in spring green. The banks were massed with grass and vegetation and the rutted lane was drying out quickly after a wet spring. Soon the hot summer days to come would find it airless and overpoweringly heavy with the heady aroma of a million wild flowers and drowsy from the soporific buzz of innumerable flies and bees.

Some fun could be had by digging out bumblebee nests and taking them back to place in boxes in the gardens, but they always died soon after.

Swiftly now, downhill towards the flour mill on the River Windrush. Past a big ash tree which Jim always associated with a crock of gold. It hadn't been fair, last year, pursuing the old adage, that there's a crock of gold at the end of a rainbow, he'd seen it bathed in a golden glow and had run right across a field, only to see the rainbow move quietly, tantalisingly away, matching the speed of his approach. Down past the kite-flying field with its newly erected electric light poles.

There had been admonitions all round. "Don't get too near those wires, you'll get killed".

The kites were heavy, ponderous fabrications made by the boys from two willow sticks tied in a crucifix shape, strung with parcel string and covered with brown paper. The tail was formed by tying on more bunches of newspaper, which could be added to if the kite had a tendency to nose-dive, or subtracted from if it flew nose up. They needed a very quick sprint into a brisk wind to get launched.

On down, the lane overhung by another row of tremendous elms which threatened to shed any dead branches when gales were blowing, to the river and the mill which was also a small holding. In the bank opposite these trees was the now disused clay pit, and farther down on the left near the river were the recently abandoned gravel pits. These names meant little to the boys, but over the years, like the local stone quarries, they had supplied the necessary aggregates for local development.

Further down stream on the Taynton road, where a rivulet is bridged in the last dip of the road was Mortar Pits; this was a dreaded spot after dark. A ghostly coach and four would sometimes appear, crossing the bridge and frightening the lonely traveller out of his wits. Another phenomenon of this kind, a lady on a white charger often crossed the road, near the bridge at the bottom of the hill leading from Great Barrington to the Fox Inn.

Reaching the gate to the mill, they met Leslie Hands and his son Philip. Leslie worked for the miller, helping in the mill and making deliveries. Philip who was a year older than Jim, won his scholarship to the grammar school a year earlier. He was an only son, with an older sister, Eileen. The sad thing is that as a bright boy he was accepted into the RAF as a navigator. Returning in a Lancaster bomber from a raid, it was intercepted by a German fighter plane as it approached its home base. All crew were killed when it was shot down. His grave, that of a nineteen-year-old, can be seen in Great Barrington cemetery. Jim attended the funeral, at which a colour party of the RAF regiment fired a gun salute. The whole village mourned and his parents never recovered from the shock.

The Mill, Great Barrington

Jim, who like Philip, trained enthusiastically with the Burford Air Training Corps, would never forget that day. On later being rejected as a potential pilot because of colour blindness, he would always console himself that, "There but for the grace of God go I."

The miller's horse stood patiently, suffering this intrusion of his Sunday break. Inured to noise, this old war-horse, who carried the scars of service in the hell of trench warfare was now content to haul the newly ground flour and to deliver incomparable lardy cakes, dough cakes and freshly baked bread around the villages. In order that the grass in the field could grow for hay, he was now confined to his stable. When it was ready to cut, he would be harnessed first in the cutter, and when it was made, he would haul it away in the big, broad hay wagon. Hay, however, does not make itself, and a motley, but cheerful crowd of men, women, boys and girls would turn it with heavy wooden rakes before pitching it into haycocks to await collection. And the sun always shone because "You can only make hay when the sun shines".

The hay wagon stood ready in its shed where it had languished since last spring. No problems of perished rubber tyres. When, through age and the battering from rutted roads, the wheels eventually collapsed, new ones would be made in the village.

Charles Long, the carpenter and the wheelwright in the lower village, would fashion and fit new wooden spokes and wheel rim. Then George Hall, the blacksmith, would make and fit a new tyre.

This encircling band of iron was hammered and shut to form a perfect circle. Its circumference was slightly less than the rim. A fierce fire fuelled with

Barrington Blacksmith, Bill Hall on the right. *Left* – Harry Cambray. *Centre* – Nell Batt of Windrush. Photo taken while helping out at Windrush Smithy

faggots of brushwood was lit under it. The tyre, then expanded by the heat, glowing red-hot, was persuaded with sledgehammers to drop onto the wooden wheel, which lay there on the tyreing pit. The whole was accomplished by George and his two sons, Bill and Jim, in a fury of activity, shrouded in smoke, showered by sparks and coloured by many generous oaths and epithets. After the steam from the cooling water had subsided, the wheel lay there, its wooden joints pulled tight by the shrinkage of the iron band, a tribute to the accuracy and artifice of the rural craftsmen. The shaping and tempering of metal was in their blood having descended from generations of smiths.

When the old horse needed to be shod, he would take his turn amongst the many others, who, haltered to the smithy door, would be cajoled, bullied and often receive resounding thumps from the shoeing hammer to keep still and not kick too enthusiastically whilst this was being done. Off came the worn out shoe, pulled away with a claw hammer, and then after the new shoe had been adjusted for size and shape, it was heated to red-hot, held in place against the hoof by long tongs and nailed into place.

The smoke, which billowed out as the hoof burnt to its shape, was peculiar to that process and can only be described as similar to the smell when a dentist uses a high-speed drill on an unfortunate tooth.

One of the most feared dates in the school calendar was the annual visit of the dentist. This entailed the evacuation of one classroom and an inspection of every pupil. In fear, the luckless infant was marched in and confronted by Mr. Wren the dentist, a high seat, a treadle drilling machine, a chipped enamel bowl and an unsmiling, aged "nurse" assistant. Tender young mouths were decimated. Bad teeth, milk teeth, slightly suspect and healthy molars all shared the same fate.

After the insistent command of, "Open wide Johnny", it could be guaranteed that either the quick pain of an extraction or two would follow or the far more scalp raising and excruciatingly painful process of having a few fillings would ensue. The treadle would revolve the drill at different speeds, the nerves would scream as the process assumed the torture of the Spanish Inquisition. To have a tooth pulled was so much more acceptable than to have one filled, even if it did entail rinsing out the mouth with an unpleasant disinfectant and having that dreadful enamel bowl stuck under one's chin to catch the resultant bloody mess.

Coats of red or yellow paint would preserve the wooden wheel from the weather, see it through years of work and maybe, into posterity.

In summer the cart shed served another purpose. The river, now clogged by silt and weed and diminished by water extraction, then afforded several choice spots for bathing, known individually as "The Girls", "The Boys" and "The Mens". No "Ladies".

Bathing and swimming were activities in which the adult ladies of the village never indulged despite the fact that there were no baths at home.

"The Girls" was a stretch below the Mill Bridge. Their modesty was preserved by changing their clothes in the dark depths of the cart shed, screened by the hay wagon. Small children also used the same spot under the watchful eyes of the young teenage girls. A useful and commendable arrangement.

Indeed one day, Jim himself had been dragged unceremoniously from the water and harshly lectured on a new and surprising fact of life. He'd been lying comfortably on the river bed, fascinated by the swirls and currents of green water passing over him and his proximity to the minnows and bullheads swimming around, when his little world was spoilt by the intrusion of bare legs and desperate, grabbing, heaving hands. After expectorating a considerable amount of river water, he was scolded and left in no doubt that he needed air to breathe and that drowning was a permanent condition.

It was in that same cart shed that, now older, he had unwittingly surprised a young nymphet. Although she quickly covered herself, the interest roused by the sight of that young female body, blessed by pert and well-developed breasts was to stay with him forever. A decade was to pass before he saw its like again.

The sluice gates had been cranked up, allowing the river to drop into the millpond. A torrent of water cascading into its unknown depths. The millrace was languid. Sunday rest was upon the mill itself. No rumble of the mill wheel, no turmoil of the millrace, a dusty miller's bag obscuring the mill window and both top and bottom panels of the stable-type door closed.

Behind it the machinery rested. The newly dressed millstones were idle and the mice undisturbed. Tomorrow the mill-race would fill, the mighty water-wheel revolve, that huge and dependable source of free power would hoist big sacks of grain to the top floor, the stones would turn and the flour would cascade down the chutes to be bagged and set aside for collection or delivery.

The mill had been worked by generations of the Griffin family since Charles Griffin married Anne Edgworth at Taynton in 1839 and took her there to live. They had six children, (George William, who died in infancy); Sarah, Mary, Hannah, Clare, Henry and Anne who was born after her father had been thrown from his horse in Priory Lane, Burford. A tragic accident from which he never recovered. He was buried in Taynton churchyard, as was his infant son. Anne, his wife, carried on the business for many years and was recognised as quite a character, as indeed she must have been. She was a Methodist and attended chapel at Windrush. Son Henry took over the running of the Mill married Ann Bew and lived in Yew Tree Cottage where Charles, the next miller was born. In due course they moved to the Mill where they had seven children; Clara, Hubert, Robert, Rhoda, Ernest, Harold and Margaret.

In September 1913, Charles Griffin returned from East Hagbourne, all of forty miles, with wagon and horses bringing all the family possessions to be reunited with his wife and very young daughters, Nancy and Margaret who had been despatched by rail to Shipton station. They stayed at the Mill for another twenty-two years.

The river and the millpond teemed with fish. Huge, lazy chub, trout rising to the flies, roach, pike and the quick grayling, shoals of minnows and stickleback and lurking under the stones, a mass of crayfish.

The Windrush was the first English river into which grayling had been introduced. As now, the fishing was completely off limits, being the preserve of the squire, but handlines baited with bread or worm and slid in quietly from a bridge parapet easily caught a couple of fish. These, wrapped in conveniently big dock leaves, to avoid the slime, could be secreted and proudly carried home. "Did you try eating Chub?" Don't. To humour their clamouring offspring, their mothers would overcome the slime, the cleaning and de-scaling of the trophy. Their best cooking efforts resulted in a bony, revoltingly earthy tasting dish. Once tried, never repeated.

Their next short walk took them over the water-meadows by way of a track raised above the flood-level to bridge a second river. This had been the river proper. The only one, until centuries before it had been breached below Windrush where a weir, now split quite half of the water into a man-made course, leading it below the mansion, enhancing the vista from the pleasure gardens; forming a wide curve called the Broad Water where swans, mallard and moorhens floated and upended to grace its smooth surface.

The iridescent flash of a kingfisher attracted their attention upstream just in time to see a big disturbance near the bank under the shade of a row of willow trees. "Did you see that? I'll bet it was an otter," said George. "I've been otter hunting up above The Fox, saw 'em catch one, bigger than our cat it was. Dogs goes swimming and paddling about in the water and some of the blokes get in there too." The others had watched but never seen one caught. The visit from the otter hounds was a rare occasion, Fox hounds yes. Regular annual meets, sometimes round the war memorial at the top of the village, but more often in front of the mansion where liveried servants could circulate and hand up their silver trays so that the mounted riders could enjoy the traditional stirrup cup.

Over the bridge they met Minnow Lane. "Which way shall us go then, right or left? I be 'aving a drink fust, any road". Taking it in turn, each boy dropped to his knees to cup his hands and scoop refreshment from the clear waters of a spring bubbling away at the confluence of the tracks.

Meet at Barrington Memorial. Mrs Wingfield talking to Huntsman at right of picture

Like oases, these springs were bliss in the summer to hot, dusty, sweaty boys, whose mouths were parched from too much shouting and spitting. They were well constructed so that the water flowed into large, stone built hollows before spilling out to form their tiny streams and chuckle along to the river.

They had served many generations of villagers whose well defined paths had compacted under the weight of countless buckets of water, carried on yokes by work-worn, ageing men, stoical, stooped and weary women or more usually, sloshing over puny legs, dragged manfully home by generations of small boys.

This spring served the mean little cottages of Minnow Lane. Another one rose in the middle of Little Barrington green. Another called the Cold Bath at the bottom of Fairford Hill, which carries the road down from Great Barrington to the stone bridge. They flowed sweetly and unfailingly throughout the year, their waters clear and cold, sustaining man and beast and the insects that hovered over them, the water boatmen that skated on them and those that lived in their depths. Fresh water snails vied with tiny silvery shrimps to further cleanse and purify this, natures' copious bounty. Many decades were to pass before alien water was piped to the villages, coinciding strangely with the declaration that all of the springs were contaminated and unfit for human consumption. "Don't believe it! Try some before it's too late."

"Well we ain't going that way", said George indicating the path to the right. "The kids have broken nearly all the windows in Whitemans' farmhouse and there's nothing else to do along that way".

That sunken pathway, under more big elm trees, which were rooted in the very wall that bounded it, had once been the main access to the village from Great Barrington. Eventually it was superseded by Strong's causeway. This is now the road, which crosses the meadows between The Fox Inn and Great Barrington.

So they turned off left, past the Bennet's house where a motorcycle was propped up the front gate.

"That's Cliff Bennet's bike. Did you know as e'd ad a bad accident, 'it a car on Leys crossroads and nearly died?"

Poor Cliff survived but was never quite right afterwards. Past Bob Tye's little cottage, like most of the others there, a one room up and one down dwelling. A sight of the occupier, sitting there smoking his churchwarden's pipe and then up to Middle Road, that narrow switch-back country lane which winds along the river valley to Burford.

Mr George Mathews of
Paper Mill Cottages

"Alright, which way be we off now then?" asked George. "Shall us go down to the Paper Mill?"

The road fell away left, to a huddle of buildings. A paper mill in rural Gloucestershire seemed then to be an anachronism, but there it still stands. The wooden slats of the drying shed surviving the centuries and there lived George Mathews, a small, bearded, gnome-like, Victorian figure, long coat, leggings and over-sized trilby hat.

"No, I'm not going that way," said Jim.

He hated passing the high roadside wall, breached by two forbidding gateways and somehow imagined he'd be caught and incarcerated by Colonel Hurst. Behind the wall stands Barrington Grove, with its commanding views of the river, where the boys would sometimes risk a bit of fishing, one eye over their shoulders in dire fright of being seen and chased off by the owner.

"He isn't really a colonel, he's a lieutenant colonel, same as Colonel Wingfield. Old Colonel Chetwynd Stapylton is what they call a full colonel. Still he can't have much money 'cos Home Farm, where he lives, belongs to Colonel Hurst!"

Colonel Chetwynd Stapylton was always a figure of fascination to all that chatted to him. He used a monocle, not particularly adroitly, as it constantly fell from his eye and dangled down near his tweed jacket. He retained one very large, long and stained front tooth, which caused a big indentation to his lower lip allowing it to salivate, dribble and spit fine spray at the unwary. He drove an Austin 12 car and was, later, unfortunate enough to back over and very seriously injure his wife as she directed his inadequate efforts to reverse it.

"Let's go up the Rye Piece, might get a bunny up there", said Sydney.

So turning right towards the church they then branched left onto the bridle path leading up to the main road.

The church was silent now, slumbering between Sunday services. It was old then. Built and subsequently dedicated in 1159 by Alfred, Bishop of Worcester. It had exercised its influence and performed its happy, sad and important duties for so long that it now withdrew gently behind the old yew trees. The colour of its stone fabric had long ago blended back to Mother Earth from whose bosom the golden limestone had once been plundered.

It was uphill now, up to the ridge and its main road. Crossing open fields, knowing that most rabbits would stay close to the woods on the left, but still exploring every tussock of grass and likely place to find a squat, that indentation scratched out in flat ground which allowed lop-eared bunnies to peep out, but withdraw without presenting a silhouette.

Breasting the first slope, they stopped and looked back down the wold. Along from the church, Church Farm, fronted by a grass tennis court where Miss Wilbraham could be seen lazing in the garden.

"Our dad says there's a priest-hole in there", "What's a priest-hole?"

No one seemed to know but Cyril ventured, "There's a big well at the back, so perhaps it's down there." On past the Reading Room, the only modern and brick building in the whole vista, was the old vicarage, the home of the Dean-Drummond family.

Jim said, "My dad hasn't got over that crash yet, he still gets lots of headaches".

All the boys knew he was referring to the recent accident when Ildica Dean-Drummond had collided with his father's van, taking off most of the bodywork, inside which, Walter Preston was crouching, holding a motor cycle. She had been first to contact his mother about the accident. Her opening, ill-chosen words on the telephone being, "Mrs. Lazenby, I think I've killed your husband".

Miss Dean Drummond's Singer car
after accident at Crossroads

Morris van after same accident

Happily, both survived, but his father's lack of equilibrium long after regaining consciousness from the blow, which had "knocked him out", caused much unhappiness at home.

Her sister, Marigold, was a prime mover in the local Girl Guides and assisted the Honourable Juliet Dutton and Miss Mary Wingfield in making a very successful troop. Their brother, Anthony, was later to catch the imagination of the nation when he evaded the Germans, but was eventually caught and incarcerated. His book "Return Ticket" relating all his experiences of sabotage behind enemy lines, his Arnhem drop, his captures, escapes and recaptures make compulsive reading. After the war, among other things, he became a national solo glider champion. As a retired Army Major-General he took the salute of the Arnhem survivors at their 50th Anniversary Parade.

On again towards the beech lined highroad. No rabbits now, these acres were for hares, those incredibly fast creatures, all long legs and tall ears. One got up, loped some thirty yards and then lowered itself into the grass again. Hopeless to try and catch it, but being boys they sped off towards the spot, where, because of its perfect camouflage, only a pair of long, twitching ears were still visible. It got up and effortlessly distanced itself again leaving the boys to finish their journey up to the main road.

They turned right making their way to the crossroads where the Barrington road meets the A40. Looking the other way, Cyril said, "It was along there that woman got murdered, chucked her body over the hedge into the field by the county border. It was Mrs. Mathews from Windrush Mill, didn't you know about it?"

Jim had never been told about this shocking event and asked for more.

"Well she was riding her bike from Burford to Windrush when some Welshman, who'd just deserted the army, stopped her and killed her for it. That's what I been told anyway. They says they got him for it. Suppose they must have hanged him cos that's what happens if you kill anybody." That such a thing could possibly have happened here seemed too enormous to digest and Jim was filled with disbelief, rejecting the thought completely. It was true.

At the crossroads two more boys were sitting on the iron rail fence, pencils and notebooks in hand, taking down the registration numbers of the cars as they passed. This was a nice steady interest, not too demanding unless two were fairly close together.

Little Barrington Church

"'Ow many you got then, Den?" asked George of Dennis Long, the wheelwright's son. "Must be about forty between us" he said glancing at his friend Ted Ball. "There's a lot of them today".

A leisurely parade of cars was moving in both directions, begging again, that age-old question, "Where do em come from and where do em go?"

Some were easy. A crash of gears and a rattle of the chain drive heralded the approach of Archdeacon Cross's Trojan. He lived in Little Barrington at Greycote, then Lord Sherborne in AD33 a registration mark which the family kept until their demise.

BARRINGTON WOMENS INSTITUTE – outside Little Barrington Reading Room

Back Row Mrs Tufnell, ?, Edie Pitts, Mrs Keylock
Middle Row Mrs Souls, Mrs Tidmarsh and Fred, Mrs Berry, Ruby Cambray, Eva Pitts, Lizzie Hall
Front Row ?, The Miss Godley's, ? Ruby Lazenby

Mrs Lazenby with the new
Bull-Nose Morris

Distinctive cars, cars easily recognisable by their shapes and features. Characteristics which proclaimed the individuality of the manufacturers and their pride in their lineage. A Vauxhall 14, like Mr. Parkinson the vicar's car, with its fluted bonnet, a Singer Bantam with its bantam mascot atop the radiator; a bull-nosed Morris, with its bulbous honeycomb radiator and its dickie-seat, two young girls sitting in there waving furiously. This was one like Jim's father had got. Given to him new as a wedding present by his father-in-law, it had survived the honeymoon in Devon and Cornwall, the rigours of a general garage workhorse and now made somewhat irregular trips to see the other grandparents in Carterton, which was referred to as Tin Town. This trip to a village whose dwellings were all bungalows, some constructed mainly of corrugated iron and wood and most of which boasted tin roofs was far removed from the familiar stone cottages of the surrounding villages. The dwellers were mainly small holders with huge gardens.

His grandfather having been head gardener at Bradwell Grove estate could still practise his skills on his own huge patch, some change perhaps, after having sixteen gardeners at his bidding. His late employer, Squire Fox, owner of Bradwell Grove, had made his family fortune up North, in the manufacture of Fox's folding umbrella frames, before retiring to be a country gentleman.

The Sunday afternoon jaunts were both happy and fraught. When it rained the dickie seat offered little protection, but a fine day was glorious, except for certain nose-wrinkling moments such as when the car turned up the Carterton road from Burford, where was sited a noisome, smoking ash tip and rubbish dump and the smell vacuumed back into the dickie.

Now two young men on motorbikes, peaked caps turned backwards, eyes goggled. One bike, an old belt-driven Dunelt, its single cylinder thudding regularly, the other, a much noisier machine with leg guards. "What's that then you?" asked John. "It's a Scott Squirrel with two cylinders and a radiator, water cooled engine, expensive bike," said Jim. "Not many of them about."

Next a large, black, shining limousine, ALX 399, with two chevrons in the radiator grille. This, another unusual make, was the Citroen Floating Power, a generous six seater with fold-up occasional seats behind the driver, being driven by Colonel Hurst. When wartime petrol rationing arrived it was too thirsty for private use and was acquired by Jim's father for a superb taxi.

Then a Ford 8 saloon, the new £100 model, black car with yellow spoked wheels. All Fords were the same colour. Didn't Henry Ford say? "They can have any colour they want, as long as it's black"? They were cheap but didn't warrant the contemporary saying, "A bit of tin and a bit of board, put it together and you've got a Ford".

Yes, there was then a lot of wood in motor cars. Plywood floorboards, ash frames and door panels with many a walnut fascia and trim.

Tom Lazenby
Walter Preston behind him
Stone Tallet Steps at rear

A grey Lanchester, the distinctive whine of its pre-select gearbox, creating an uncomprehending interest, an open top Austin 7 with both the drivers' trilby hat and his streaming moustache in danger of ending up in the lap of the driver of the diminutive three-wheeled Morgan following him.

"That's Arnold Wright from Windrush", one shouted as the busy little machine, two wheels at the front and one under its tapered rear end bumbled past, its fully exposed twin engine chattering away.

"This un coming, aint alf a going" said George. It was a little red MGJ2. "Burr on it you" was the encouraging cry from the watching boys, which translated meant, "bear on the throttle man". It's doubtful the exuberant young man or his tense girlfriend received the message. The little sports car, hood and windscreen down, was being pushed close to its limit, its tiny overhead camshaft engine generating a head of steam and a plume of exhaust smoke, the pungent odour of which proclaimed that the owner could afford to use that most distinctive of engine lubricants, Castrol R.

Why can't we still have cars whose windscreens fold down to the bonnet? A most modest speed produced a breath-taking exhilaration. With hair wind-whipped, streaming eyes near shut and lips clenched tight to counter the clouds of small flies, conversation was limited to short, shouted observations. And what a way to keep awake and sober up fast after a comprehensive pub-crawl or a late energetic night with the current girlfriend. Who needed breath analysers then?

The motorised pub-crawl helped to re-vitalise the lonely inns. Cars may have been few and far between, but four or five thirsty lads, including the driver, could average eight to ten pints of beer apiece, see the countryside, sort out the pub with the best and noisiest sing-song going and still get home without endangering other members of the species.

Rabbits and hares were fair game; the roads teemed with them. Rabbits cross roads but hares run fast along them. The modern car suffers impact damage but the veterans of the thirties, high slung, with solid axle beams, provided the ultimate death trap. Large running boards and deep wing valances could accommodate the harvest of the resulting mayhem. Not a pretty sight!

And why did most people prefer to make for the most crowded tavern? Small bar rooms packed with folk, a barrier of sound, pushed and shoved from every angle, shouted conversations imperative.

"Hey landlord, we're next."

"Sorry sir, chaps up the end been waiting ten minutes."

"So've we, been 'ere ages."

"Watch your backs, nearly had my beer down your neck."

"You're lucky, you've got one."

"Well why don't you sod off down to The Bell?"

"Sod that after waiting all this time and with all that talent in the other room, not bloody likely, it's good 'ere."

"Thank God, at last Jack, double order now you're there, line 'em up on top of the piano, and one for the pianist".

Winter nights were the busiest. The bucolic locals, relieved of the pressures of harvest and gardening, were able to indulge the pleasure of darts, shove-halfpenny, dominoes and song singing. Saturday night was over-crowded with youngsters imbibing enough Dutch courage to face the rigours and embarrassment of dances in the many local village halls. Most of the lads would be wallflowers, unable to dance but there to study and discuss form among themselves. The unfortunate girls, dancing in pairs, often under the wary eyes of their formidable mothers must, from the furtive looks and snatches of overheard conversations indulged in by the semi-inebriate boys, have felt themselves akin to the young heifers in the ring at the local cattle market.

What a sad indictment of man's progress that now, again, the isolated country inns and pubs are quiet and that the village hall dance has disappeared, to be replaced by frantic discos, which in turn have had to cease because of the emergence of violence and thuggery.

Leaving now, the lads gravitated to the area at the back of the inn a couple of hundred yards to their right, an old coaching inn which now stood isolated, bereft of its past importance.

The Barrington New Inn, the benchmark on it denoting six hundred and twenty feet above sea level had been one of the regular and necessary stops for coaches on the Gloucester to London run. A change of horses, a pint of local ale or a glass of porter and an exchange of news had been good for business and good for the constitution.

The Coaching Inn, long after, rechristened The Inn for all Seasons, had died, victim to the railways, charabancs, cars and the 30's depression. It's fabric in disrepair, the cobblestones grass grown, the barns, coach houses, stables and other accommodation silent and deserted. Small wonder that one member of the Whitlock family, who'd been there for generations had hanged himself from a beam in the tallet. There was always an uncomfortable feeling after ascending those stone steps leading to it.

The area to the east and the rear of the inn was sure to provide sport. Neither a meadow nor even a field it's known as Little Barrington Quarry banks. Not to be confused with Great Barrington Quarry banks, a similar area immediately above the deer park, but now a flat somewhat sunken field by the sheep dip. It was flattened by American forces during their long stay, preparatory to their D.Day landings when they employed their D.4s and D.8s, graders and heavy plant to level it for a vehicle park. The sheep-dip served as an inspection pit and grease bay.

Several acres of unnatural hillocks, small valleys, miniature scree slopes and crevasses, part wooded and part covered with short, springy grass. Rabbit warrens abounded, cowslips, cornflowers and butterflies created a haven for wildlife and young boys alike.

It's said that time heals all. The now peaceful environment must have presented a far more noisy and unpleasant scene when these very roods were being raped to supply the incomparable limestone, which went to the building of Sir Christopher Wren's cathedral of St. Pauls. Quarrymen, masons, hauliers and teams of horses alike must have strained and sweated to prise out, shape and prepare huge blocks of soft limestone for transportation to London. A hard life, but one which must have been welcome to the local economy and to the local inns in particular.

Overseen too by the master masons of the Strong family, the same ones that had built the causeway, had lived in the village and had built the house at and wrested stone from Kitts Quarries near Burford. They played a large part in the erection of the wonderful cathedral itself.

Each local hamlet and village had its own quarry; the houses were built from them. Some, like Taynton and Farmington are still worked, stone for the Oxford colleges, the majority lie dormant under a mantle of grass. Most were open workings, but others like Windrush were mined. The soft mined stone was superb for working and carving but weathered badly, as evidenced by the way that the tombstones in Windrush churchyard have split and sharded over the centuries. The mine tunnel still exists there; even some of the trams and tramlines but all is now screened by a mature stand of trees. At this time of writing, Nicholas Parsons, the radio and T.V. presenter, lives under their shadow in the mine manager's cottage.

Entering Quarry Banks from the gateway just down the hill, the boys, quite unaware of the significance of the terrain, knowing only that the estate still quarried stone just in on their left, made haste to acquire some rabbiting sticks from the back of the hedge. Armed with sharp shut knives or pocket-knives, they quickly selected and trimmed out suitable, strong, three-foot long wands. "Watch out Jim, watch out where you be a treading", was Cyril's sudden caution. With revolting disgust Jim saw that he had been about to step in a quite colossal stool, which a very large man must have been relieved to deposit behind the hedge. Cyril's further comment seemed to be particularly apt, "By God" he said, "I'll bet that didn't alf make his eyes sparkle".

Although the prevailing wind usually blew towards them they whetted a fore-finger, stuck it up in the air to check which side got cold, decided their scent would be left behind them and with the cunning and stealth of well-practised hunters, divided, some to flush the rabbits from their squats and others to head them off as they headed for their buries or warrens. Those to the left took to the high ground, well back into the field, working their way round unseen, some to drop down and take advantage of any cover near the burrow entrances.

No words were spoken, simple signs sufficing. A cautious hand raised by a boy on the high ridge indicated where he could see a bunny, ears twitching, sunning itself in a tuft of grass on the valley floor. Another boy, keeping downwind, worked his way towards it. Then with a quick rush he bounded forward and with a well-aimed swipe knocked the rabbit sideways. Falling on it he then rose triumphantly, squealing rabbit in hand, to administer the coup de grace. This was quick and simple. Hind legs held, thumb and forefinger either side of the neck, a quick jerk and the quarry was dead in a second. No word had yet been spoken and the boys continued their hunt.

Most rabbits, now on their guard, escaped easily, disappearing down holes with that thumping sound, peculiar to them, the little white scut under their tails being the last sign seen of them. Others gave a chase. One, finding its own home blocked, took off in another direction, followed by two boys who were thwarted when it bolted through a large clump of stinging nettles and squeezed into a well-blocked up and well camouflaged tunnel entrance.

This was the tunnel, beautifully constructed, with arch-stoned roof, which led directly into the cellar of the pub some hundred yards away. The reason for labouring to construct such a perfect and considerable project is still a matter for conjecture. Was it for egress or ingress? Surely not for the quarry men to slink off and have a quick pint unseen by their masters! A super priest's hole! An exit for highwaymen after plundering the coaches on the old high road. What?

The regular beat of an exhaust could now be heard issuing from a pipe poking through the wall of a large stone coach-house and stable block, part of the hostelry complex. It let most of the fumes escape from the big single cylinder Drake and Gorham petrol, paraffin engine which powered the recently installed 50 volt D.C. lighting plant.

Two years ago, Willy Whitlock, the inn tenant, had fallen victim to the ravages of the thirties financial depression and had found it necessary to hand in his notice to the property owner, the Barrington Estate.

THE NEW INN

The New Inn Near Great Barrington

Jim's father applied for it and found himself with "A licence to sell Tobacco, beer, wines and spirits for six days only." The six days only requirement was common to all three inns owned by the estate. Neither The Barrington New Inn, The Fox Inn or The Merrymouth Inn could open on a Sunday. This was never seriously questioned and flaunted, only by a select band of back door visitors who were entertained in the rear parlours.

So there it was, Thomas William Lazenby, publican. A most unlikely landlord, never a drinker, no time for it and a wife, Ruby, who'd probably never been into a local in her life.

This situation arose because Tom wished to establish a garage on the main road. He had begun an automotive repair business in the yard and garage building attached to his home near the war memorial in Great Barrington. Such was the disturbance created by the testing of noisy motor cycle engines, the straightening of bent motor cars and the continuous running of a small electric plant, which allowed him to work into the small hours, as well as to charge up the many glass, wet cell, two volt wireless accumulators belonging to those villagers who could afford a wireless set, that his application was regarded favourably, and presumably, with great relief. He had no intention of becoming a publican and so arranged affairs that "Buller" Whitlock should remain as "mine host" thereby allowing himself to develop the yard and its many buildings into a general repair area with petrol pumps.

Three large holes were dug to accommodate three big, heavy petrol tanks, each capable of containing fully five hundred gallons, a major improvement after having to dispense petrol in sealed two gallon cans delivered from the Shell depot at Stow-on-the-Wold. Rumour has it that the chaps who dug them, Fred Russell and Walter Preston, were handsomely rewarded with a couple of pints of beer.

The second hand lighting plant was installed, its twenty-six big glass cell batteries hoisted to and bedded down in the upstairs loft and wired to three new Wayne pumps. These were the first electric petrol pumps in a ten-mile radius. Naturally over the years the engine had to be replaced, the lead cell batteries buckled and split, raining streams of acid down through the already decrepit floorboards and making life hazardous in the extreme. The glass-cased mercury switch at the base of the control board burnt up its contacts in showers of orange sparks, requiring frequent top ups with quicksilver mercury. The long, flapping driving belt between the engine and the dynamo broke with alarming regularity, smashing anything within reach, but thankfully missing all human targets for whom there was no protection. The starting handle, crude and fearsome, had a nasty habit of kicking back; flying off and maiming all those who tried to master it.

"Let's go and play in your dad's old cars" said Cyril.

With misgiving, Jim replied "OK but you'd better keep out of his sight or he'll tell me off when I get home."

They had now reached a wide track, which served both as a means of getting loaded wagons down from the farm buildings to the lower pastures and as a path to the village. Mostly defined by stone walls, it wound round the cover and skirted another tree-lined quarry hole. This was useful not only as a rubbish dump but was the stinking outfall for the inn sewage pipe.

The top of the track widened out into the old farmyard, which now held an array of derelict cars and one old Reo horsebox. A couple of straight eight Buicks, a small Swift, a Clyno and a couple of bullnosed Morris's rusting away. Others were pushed into the disused cattle sheds and even into the big Cotswold hay barn. When the car doors were opened for the lads to play, there was a pervading smell of mildewing fabric and rotting wood, their plate-glass windscreens were going green from the water dripping off the big spreading chestnut tree, while weeds and corn sprouted from every crevice.

"Is that where that black man lives?" asked Cyril, indicating the old horsebox.

"Yes, but don't go by it he might be there" said Jim.

Much interest had been aroused when a big black man had arrived in the locality. Augustus Olat Okumbo Gabriel Cole was the first that most had ever seen. He'd been unable to find lodgings and

Jim's father had let him set up home there. Incredibly, to them, he was a highly educated man, a civil engineer involved in building Little Rissington aerodrome. He could be seen riding a big bicycle to work every day and was in charge of some of the local labour.

"What's he like then?"

"He's ever so nice and kind."

"They say's as their hands be white on the palms, is that right?"

"Yes, perhaps you'll see when he comes out."

"Why has he got a name like that, do you think he's any relation to the Cole family down the village?"

All agreed it seemed highly unlikely, but puzzled over the question for a while. Olat later moved into a couple of draughty rooms over the workshop.

Further up the yard a youth was washing a car.

"Who's that then?" came the inevitable question.

"That's Matty Sokolov, works for my dad, he's a White Russian."

"What do you mean, a White Russian, are there some black ones?"

"Well, his parents had to run away when there was a revolution out there and Mr. Bell, a farmer from Shilton asked dad to give him a job."

This was true but the poor chap, born of a gentile family, with impeccable manners, good education and a richly modulated voice, was treated so badly that Jim's mother often implored her husband to go more easily on him. He cycled from Shilton in all weathers and was given all the oily and mucky jobs attendant to such a crude establishment. He bore them with a resigned and philosophical fortitude. In such a parochial situation, a White Russian and a black African were quite a novelty.

A car pulled up at the front, next to the Cleveland Discol pump. The other pumps, easily distinguishable by their varied shaped glass domes were National Benzole and Shell.

A pair of legs issuing from under a Ford lorry on which was the legend, R Oakey, Hay and Straw, Transport. Alvescot, struggled to extricate Jim's father. With overalls shining with layers of oil and grease, black oil on his head and hands dripping more of it, he emerged from his task of fitting new big ends to a well-worn crankshaft. He grabbed an oily rag and wiping his hands furiously, hurried to serve the patient customer.

This was worth watching. The petrol cap in front of the windscreen unscrewed, the pump hose lifted off, the sight glass on top of the petrol pump agitating and a whole three gallons being delivered.

This completed, the driver shouted out "You haven't drained the hose."

No good assuring him that it didn't apply to the modern pump which had a trigger valve at its delivery end, so best to make much of the lifting of the hose above the tank filler and keep him happy. Maybe he'd only been to hand operated pumps before where a cupful might well stay in the pipe.

"That will be three shillings and fourpence halfpenny, sir."

Discol was one of the more expensive brands and was at that time selling for one shilling and three halfpence a gallon. What a lot of money that seemed when the farm labourer's wage might start at thirty shillings a week to keep a family.

After peeping into the workshop where the big electric plant was banging and slapping away they retreated down the yard. A big open Lagonda stood near the workshop building, its prominent red triangle on its rear bumper proclaiming, "Four Wheel Brakes", a suitable warning to owners of older cars that their two wheel brake system would be sorely tried if they were too near to it when it stopped. It was the garage hack, having been used, Jim assisting, to transport all the tools and equipment to their present location as well as serving as a tow truck, rescuing many stranded vehicles. Mechanical breakdowns were common place in those evolving years.

Back now down the track and into the heavily tree-grown area of the quarry. It yielded nothing, the snapping of dead undergrowth warning the wildlife that danger was approaching. The scutter of dead leaves as rabbits moved, the explosion of sound as pigeons rushed out of the trees and the sudden squawk and drum of its wings as a cock pheasant propelled itself from the wood-side, were as familiar as the sight of red squirrels leaping for shelter high in the branches.

It's not easy to watch a squirrel as it climbs a treetrunk. When you are on one side he will be round the other. By walking round the base he can be made to go round in circles, stopping sometimes to peer back round to see where you are.

A pigeon could be heard high in the beeches at the end of the wood, its plaintive but soothing call echoing down the green caverns, "My toe bleeds, Betty, my toe bleeds Betty", answered by another from the ivy-clad tree down to the left and then another and another.

Come sundown these lofty fastnesses would welcome back a whole populace of birds. Marauding pigeons, crops full from the fields of the poor tenant farmers, despite the effort of the "clapper boys" who'd been paid a pittance to stand around banging and rattling to keep them off. Chattering jackdaws and stealthy crows who'd survived the gamekeeper's onslaught when he shot the high nests away, after the eggs were laid. A cacophony of cock pheasants seeming determined to call attention to their present whereabouts, their calls, slowly subsiding into an occasional cluck as they, like the pigeons, huddled tight against the trunks of dark firs or hid in the ivy which seemed determined to strangle the very trees to which it clung, would soon leave the wood cloaked in silence.

Come darkness, the quietness would be shattered by the cries of a dog fox and the rustle of the badger family as it emerged from its cavernous sett.

Jim's mind cast back to last autumn when he'd nearly been shot by his father. Employing all the imagined stalking skills of the Red Indians gleaned from his boyhood reading, he'd set out to find dad, who, armed with his old twelve bore hammer gun was somewhere in the wood, patiently waiting for the returning pigeons. Avoiding every dead twig that might crack underfoot, skirting around hollows filled with dead leaves and worming through tangles of fallen undergrowth he'd come within some ten yards of the motionless figure, silhouetted against the fading evening sky before he was seen. His father's concern and his forcibly expressed agitation that he might have been shot in mistake for a rabbit was a lesson he'd remember for a lifetime.

Emerging from the end of the wood, the boys negotiated a barbed wire fence, from which hung a familiar, but always grisly collection. Tied to it, moving slightly in the breeze, were the remains of rooks, magpies, stoats and even a jay whose best feathers would now be adorning the sweaty, trilby hatband of George Hill, the under-keeper. How much impression this made on the remaining vermin can't be assessed, but it served well to prove that the man was executing his job to the satisfaction of the head keeper and the squire.

Still on quarried ground, the boys advanced, avoiding dense patches of stinging nettles which thrived in the open spaces under a couple of stands of magnificent mature beeches, to check the last of the excavations which were riddled with more rabbit warrens. Fresh cartridge cases were littered around, evidence that someone was enjoying rook pie. The remains of nests and eggs strewed the ground.

"Come on, let's climb some of these trees," said George. "I'm going to carve my name up there again."

Some of the trees, of huge girth, branched out low down and afforded ideal perches and vantage points. The trees climbed, penknives were soon opened and initials carved deep into the smooth beech bark. Over the years they would distort and fill but the sometimes decipherable scars would always remain. AG–BM with a carved heart pierced by an arrow.

Descending, the boys, ignoring the rabbit warren, scouted around to locate any pop holes. These are short tunnels scratched out by wary rabbits who, seeing their main escape route cut off can go to ground in an emergency. Ingenious maybe, but with no escape, a sort of bunnies cul-de-sac. Into these, the broken fibrous end of the rabbiting sticks were inserted. On meeting any obstruction, which might or might not be the end of the hole, they were revolved several times and then withdrawn for inspection. Finding a wealth of "flick" – rabbit fur – on the rough end, which had obviously been pushed against and wound hard into a petrified bunny, jackets came off, sleeves were rolled up and skinny arms thrust shoulder-deep into the hole so that practised hands could grab and extricate the squealing denizen. Something like conjuring a rabbit out of a hat but with a rather more sinister ending. If lucky, there might be two or three in there, jammed in like sardines. In fact it wouldn't be altogether unusual for a keeper or a beater on a mixed shoot to take eight or ten rabbits out of the same hole.

Tiring of this sport and having added another two trophies to their collection, the "gang" now sat or stretched out on the grassy hillocks to sun themselves.

George, the inveterate poacher, then fished out his treasured hocking knife and deftly proceeded to deal with five dead rabbits. Three were in wonderful condition, three quarters grown and would be tender in the frying pan. The folding knife, razor sharp, with a curved and pointed blade was used dextrously to slit down the belly to allow the paunch to drop out, a somewhat bloody and smelly operation and then for hocking the animal. This consists of making a slit between bone and sinew in one back leg thereby allowing the other to be pushed through, thus forming a convenient crux for carrying, either by the fore finger or stick.

When haymaking and harvest seasons arrived these same boys would be seen two at a time, Indian file, shouldering each end of a six-foot stick, from which half a dozen floppy carcasses would swing their way home.

Having dealt with the first three, George, with some disdain, picked up a nice, fat full-grown rabbit.

"This un's no good Jim, it's a milky old doe" and to demonstrate, zipped the knife up its middle and shook out, not just the entrails, but six well grown young which would soon have been feasting on the already distended teats. With a flourish, he whirled it around his head and slung it far into the bottom of the nettle filled quarry.

"Keep that stoat we seen, busy for a bit."

Carrion crows would probably be first on the scene to enjoy the heaps of bloody paunch.

The last rabbit fared little better.

"Don't want this un either, it's a stinking old buck, tough as can be. Still I'll take im home for our dad's ferrets, shan't bother to paunch him though, let em get in there themselves. Ad a bad days ferreting yesterday, our dad had I sweating on the graft for hours".

The graft was the long, narrow-bladed spade specially made for digging down into rabbit holes and warrens.

"We was doin' that big bury down the bottom end of Long Robin."

Everyone knew where he was talking about; Long Robin was the name of a field up behind the village. Every field is still referred to by name, whose origins go back through the centuries. Some, self-explanatory like Quarry Ground, but others such as White Sicky, Cats Brain and Long Robin being totally obscure. Similarly, all the woods are named but most disclose their origins, Mill Copse, Budget and Coronation for instance.

"We 'adn't bin there no time, got all the nets down with Jack, our old terrier waiting. Puts in two ferrets, three rabbits bolts out into the nets and then nothing. They two bitches 'ad cornered a bunny and was stuck down there a yetting (eating) it. Trouble is, when they've 'ad enough they curls up and sleeps it off. Well, dad says to put the liner in".

The liner was the big dog ferret in a separate box, which, like the other heavy one, had to be slung across the back and carried through muddy ploughing and hoisted over fence and wall. It was called the liner because it wore a collar to which a long cord was attached and when it was sent in to find the bitches, the line was paid out until it stopped. From this could be deduced both the distance which it had travelled and hopefully, the direction it had taken.

The next move would be to try and calculate where to start digging so as to retrieve all three ferrets. This often entailed hours of hard and careful work, the idea being to get straight down to them, but make sure that neither the line was severed nor that the graft injured the precious ferrets. A very daunting task, particularly when the holes were situated under the edge of a high bank or amongst rough bramble and thorny shrubs. Worse still if the line had caught around a tree root and stopped the liner yards away from its goal.

"And ee stopped down there too, so by the time we got 'em out we'd 'ad enough and made off 'ome".

George now spreadeagled himself out on the bank. Shiny drops of blood were starting to dry into his patched shirt. His short trousers adorned with two large patches on his rump slid back up to his white thighs contrasting to his muddy and bloody legs. Like all of them, his knees were heavily scarred and displayed the newest scratches and scabs from everyday contact with brambles, barbed wire and road stone chippings. None of them would graduate to long trousers until they left school at fourteen. No protective socks adorned his legs, which were stuck into a pair of big scruffy hob-nailed boots. Lying there, the boots seemed to dominate the wearer, but scant attention was paid to the fact that both soles had big holes in them. The thicknesses of cardboard which his father, like many others, had shaped and fitted inside were wearing through and the black sole of one foot could be seen. George, now content, stretched, laced his fingers behind his head, closed his eyes and nodded off.

Knowing smiles and glances suddenly appeared on the other faces as each one saw that Cyril had produced his burning glass and was directing the suns rays onto George's bare forearm. With a frantic movement he jerked upright and slapped his arm.

"Christ, something's bitten I."

He cursed and looked for the offending creature.

"Must a bin one of they emmets nests" suggested Cyril.

Emmets, or red ants, always seemed to appear as if by magic and attack with some ferocity.

"Twasn't no emmett, could a bin one of them adder snakes and they says that you can die from that" cried George.

Then recognising the innocent smiles around him and catching the glint of glass he shouted at Cyril "I'll have thee next time you bugger. Where didst thee get that there burning glass from?"

It was an example of the most prized of burning glasses.

"Came out of our dad's old carbide lamp, ee don't know I've got it yet."

With the advent of battery cycle lamps the carbide lamp was now redundant. The lamp was still self contained, but required to be kept filled with carbide powder which gave off enough fumes to ignite a small flame when water was added. The light from the flame was then concentrated through the front lens, which was also a powerful domed magnifying glass. Motorcycles needed more light and the lamp was fed by a tube from a carbide generator affixed to the frame. When the water supply ran out it was commonly accepted that the easiest way to top it up, out on a dark country road, was to pee in it. The result may have been an enhanced light. The lady pillion passenger had little option but to acknowledge the predicament.

Now, the glass with its brass rim round it was a prized possession. It could start fires from paper or dead grass, light a dog end or more often than not encourage the owner to lean forward over the school desk and concentrate the sun on an unsuspecting neck in the next row. Confiscation of this treasure could ensue. Other boys were fair game for this treatment. For the girls with their long hair, another torture was devised. A long head of timothy grass was stripped of its seeds and then gently placed against their tresses and twisted until the hair was well caught, so that with a sharp tug, several hairs parted company from the scalp and produced a scream of genuine anguish.

Looking up into the trees, alive with small birds, George, in pensive mood volunteered "Our dad says it's a pity as they bin stopped from using they clapper nets, 'ee says as lark pie was good eating".

Puzzled, Jim pursued this titbit of conversation and discovered that there were still some long fine nets on poles down in the village and that they had, until recently, been used either side of hedgerows to catch small birds startled out by clappers.

"Well how ever many sparrows and little birds would you have to catch to be worthwhile? Must be a lot and fancy having to pluck them all."

It seemed incredible to him, but then, Old King Cole had feasted on four and twenty blackbirds baked in a pie. He doubted these birds would ever sing again as in the nursery rhyme.

The view north across the valley was magnificent. The rich greens of late spring, hedges, trees, grasslands and cornfields shimmering in the sun, the limestone walls, barns and houses bathed in a warm glow.

Dominating the scene on the far side of the valley was the "Park House" set in its vast acres of wooded parkland. An imposing pile from whose family emanated all the dictates of husbandry, behaviour and the very pattern of all local life. As they owned the huge tracts of land as far as the eye could see in most directions, so did they control and nurture all the inhabitants. Small, insignificant and far away as the boys were, yet they imagined that either by field glasses or telescope they would come under the disapproving and affronted scrutiny of the revered squire.

Indeed, the area where they now were was called Pillar Ground, so named after the big gates, flanked by imposing carved and crested pillars, which gave access to the main highway. A private, tree-lined coach-road then led straight down the valley. It crossed the village road to continue by way of another gravelled riverside drive, a small picturesque bridge and a last haul up the parkland slope to the Big House. There was an uninterrupted view of a coach's impending arrival. One assumes that a member of the household staff would be kept posted to herald its approach so that the minions would be on station to serve, obey and dance attendance on its occupants.

Adding to this impression of size and grandeur were all the outbuildings built round a central yard; these included the laundry, the indoor tennis court, the stables, the dairy and the coach houses, all now serving as garages for a small fleet of motor cars. To complement all this, the old parish church of St. Mary the Virgin, which had escaped the devastation of the dreadful fire that had destroyed the previous residence centuries before, stood out clearly; partly screened by ancient yew trees. A fluttering flag of St. George was atop its flagpole high on the sturdy bell tower. A high wall separated it and the headstone-strewn graveyard from the Big House pleasure gardens to the west and the kitchen gardens to the east.

Smoke issued lazily from a couple of the many high chimneys on the mansion, fuelled from the tons of hardwood blocks which had seasoned in the outhouses, been split and wheeled in by George Berry.

The Park House, Great Barrington

Smoke too from the kitchen garden where the boiler was maintaining the temperature in the hot houses. A flash of reflected sunlight suggested that Fred Sweet, the head gardener, or one of his several under-gardeners had decided that some of the exotic plants were getting too hot and opened some of the heavy vents. This was a noisy operation, achieved by cranking a handle attached to a series of chains, shafts and gears.

Soon the prized fruit, peaches, nectarines, plums and apples would fall prey to marauding wasps. This would signal the need to destroy all the local nests. An intriguing and time consuming job, evidenced by the sight of Fred and Ernie Cambray stalking the paddocks, kneeling down in the grass and watching overhead to see the flight of the wasps. When, at last they were traced, a small bottle containing arsenic, was secured to the end of a long stick, thrust into the entrance and the wasps were instantly dispatched.

A figure could be distinguished moving around the gravelled frontage on the other side of the house. It was probably George Berry again, patiently smoothing out the wheel traces with a stout besom. The besom, that useful broom made by binding a bunch of strong twigs around a central hazelnut shaft, was ideal for this daily task. The eye wandered on up to the pigeon house, a round, domed Gothic building sited in the centre of the Deer Park.

"Queer lookin' place that, ain't it?" said George. "Why's it called a pigeon house?" "Well" said Cyril, "'cos it is a pigeon house, ain't you ever been in there? I did, last wood-picking time".

This last was a reference to the day each year, when, after the ravages of winter winds, the park gates were thrown open and the villagers were allowed in to gather up the brushwood and branches lying all over the place. This was womens' work, who, assisted by their sons and daughters, pushed and shoved home-made wheel barrows, big old prams and ingenious pram-wheeled box carts through muddy, rutted gateways, liquid cow pats and masses of deer droppings. Saws, axes or such tools were not allowed and the strength of these stalwart ladies was well tested in breaking up the firewood into transportable lengths.

The first ones in hastily threw together the nearest, biggest and best pieces into heaps, tied on a coloured rag to declare ownership and passed on to collect more. When they'd made sufficient stacks they quickly piled up their transport, tied the load on and made their first journey home. Empty, these vehicles with narrow wheels, were difficult enough, but the added weight pushed them down well into the soft going. Out came lengths of rope and string, which were tied to the front, and the youngsters of all ages were called upon to pull manfully while Mum pushed. The odd billhook was sometimes secreted and the occasional chopping noise detected behind a babble of voices raised high to disguise it.

The billhook, that most convenient tool, cross between an axe and a fagging hook, is none the less a fearsome weapon, short handle with a heavy, curved blade terminating in a wicked sharp point. Most useful when used for hedge-laying, trimming out cuttings to be used as poles for runner beans and splitting up the kindling wood.

Not to be trusted to small boys. Jim had watched incredulously when Tom Jennings had taken a swing with one, the point of which pierced his thigh, whence oozed, not only blood, but white, globules, which everyone supposed to be bone marrow.

Some of the heaviest timber defied their best efforts and so Dad was instructed to fetch it when he got back from work.

"Thee casn't miss it, it's the pile on the right just inside the gates with the bit of blue rag tied on it."

The best pickings were well across the park under 'the double beeches', a twin row of mature beech trees near to the pigeon house. It would be quite against the spirit of wood-picking to venture into it.

"I ain't never seen no pigeons in there" volunteered Sidney, "Not even coming out of all they holes round the top."

Showing his knowledge, gleaned from some obscure source, John proceeded to explain.

"Well years ago only gentry 'ad pigeons and they built places like that for them. It's perfectly round inside and there's lots of high nesting places built into the walls at different heights. There's a big post up the centre, with long, wooden steps stuck out from it. When they wanted to get to the nests built in the holes, they just 'ad to climb up and someone at the bottom could move them round just by pushing, the whole thing revolved. They could get the eggs, but what they was really after was the squabs. Squabs be young pigeons as ain't enough feathers on to fly".

"Gaw'd, couldn't fancy that," said George, "I'd rather have some pheasants eggs or a good young rabbit."

This wood wasn't the only fuel available. To augment the coal, which, at about a shilling a hundredweight was too expensive to squander, there were twice yearly deliveries of free faggots. Faggots were neatly tied bundles of brushwood. They were delivered by horse and cart to every house and were a result of the tidying and trimming of Barrington Bushes.

Barrington Bushes is a large area of woodland situated south-east of Rissington Aerodrome. It is understood that at one time the villagers had common rights to it but that the estate on the promise of regular deliveries of firewood annexed it. Like the Deer Park it was out of bounds except for Primrosing Day.

Primrosing Day was Good Friday and the annual pilgrimage to The Bushes was a highlight and special delight to the children. The woods were carpeted with primroses which were picked in their thousands to be bunched and placed in the church en masse. Window ledges, altar steps, organ niches and all other handy nooks and crannies proclaimed the wonder of nature and the dedication of the flock. While exploring the delights of the woodland, it was always surprising to come on a clearing with a small stream by which nestled a keeper's cottage. In the sun-dappled shade it looked delightful but must have been dreadfully lonely in its isolation.

"Rabbits, I hates rabbits" continued George, "Always have done since that un nearly drowned I."

Apart from its extraordinary content, this statement would seem to explain his unceasing quest to exterminate the species. Though the others seemed to be conversant with this near disaster, it escaped Jim's knowledge.

"That's stupid", he said, "A rabbit can't drown anyone."

"Well it nearly did, anyway and I'll tell you how" said George, warming to the subject. "Last harvest time some of us were sitting on the memorial wall when Cottage and Fish came up the street with their rabbiting sticks."

Cottage Clifford, so named because of his sturdy build – built like a cottage – and Fish Preston so named because of his fish eyed look.

"We said to, 'em, 'where bist thee off to?' and they says they was just a going to the field down by the brook 'cos they was just a finishing binding down there".

Binders were the horse drawn reapers which cut the corn, tied it then threw it out in sheaves ready for stacking. They were superseded in the early forties by mechanical harvesters, which not only cut the corn but threshed it too. So binders went out and what came to be known as 'combinders' came in. Most of the early combines were quite small and powered by a shaft drive from the tractor, which towed them. There was a platform on the back to accommodate an operator. His job was to bag up the corn as it came out of a shutter-operated shoot directly from the threshing drum. This was a really dusty job, made worse when barley was being harvested, as the barley "hales", prickly bits of the winnowed chaff, penetrated and irritated all skin whether protected or otherwise.

Baggy Timms, a much liked, young, farm-worker from Windrush, who was killed whilst crossing the A40 road, owed his nickname to this unpleasant task.

"Any road, there was always a lot old buzzacks down there."

Buzzacks was a very local name for rabbits.

"So we goes home and fetches our sticks and gets off to see. Well they'd only got about twenty rounds left to do".

The fields being harvested in ever decreasing circles, the rabbits naturally gravitated nearer and nearer to the centre before having to eventually break cover and run. That is to say all those who

LITTLE BARRINGTON

Little Barrington Village Green (pre-war)

LITTLE BARRINGTON

Frank Jones house on right

were not unfortunate enough to have their legs amputated by the clattering cutter blade as it moved to and fro inside the cutter bar.

"Benny Sollis was a riding the binder".

This was an uncomfortable metal seat atop the machine from which the horses' reins could ensure that the cutter reached into the crop to cut the desired swathe.

"There was old Jennings and George Hills top side of the field".

The guns usually took the upside as rabbits, like hares, with their longer rear legs seem to prefer an up gradient.

"Then there was about ten of us a watching the rest of it. We was a waiting for the bunnies to run out, a stepping into the corn just ahead of the binder, where they were creeping about, hitting a few, picking em up and jumping back quick enough so as not to get our legs cut off".

A very stupid and hazardous thing to do. If the man riding the binder had to pull up his horse because some over enthusiastic boy was about to be cut down in size, he was less than pleased.

"Then just as ee was a getting up to me Benny gives a nod and out shoots a bunny. Off I goes after him a hollering lu, lu, lu cos that seems to scare em and make em dive under the sheaves, which as you know makes it simple. All you has to do then is fall on the sheaf and put your hand under to fetch him out. I was a running after him, still shouting lu, lu, lu, ee shoots off sideways and I keeps on going straight into the brook. So there I was, couldn't swim, lying on the bottom, a watching the minnows a paddling about. Any road Preston sin I go in, but dost thee know, as if Fish adn't hooked I out, I'd a bin there still".

"Time we was off home," said John, "which way be we going, back across Pump ground and down across the Sheppey, come out of the kissing gate by The Fox?" Taking their rabbits they crossed Pump ground and headed down the well-worn path towards The Fox Inn.

Quickly Jim said, "I'm not going that way, look at all those bullocks running about".

"They things won't hurt thee, they've only got a touch of the "bry", John assured him. Even so, Jim was quite adamant, the beasts were charging fast round the field, probably irritated by flies and when they really had got the "bry", he wouldn't trust them.

"OK let's go through Little Barrington then" it was conceded.

Over a stone stile, the path branched right, across a field down to the lower village. "Shush, hold on a minute, there's a rabbit sat over there", said the ever-vigilant George, "Perhaps ee's in a wire".

It always gave him a kick to find someone else's snared rabbit, which he had for himself and then pocketed the snare for his own use. These wires or snares, consisted of a loop of pliable, stranded, copper wire with a length of whipcord securing them to a wooden peg, which was pushed well into the ground and were in common use. They were set head-high in a rabbit's run and as soon as the luckless animal pushed its head through it, the running loop tightened round its neck and hopefully strangled it there and then. Often enough when the height had been mis-judged or the snare had been disturbed, the poor thing got caught by its leg and ran round and round for hours. Many were the cats, themselves out hunting, which perished this way or were later seen on three legs having bitten through the snared one to free themselves. The same amputation frequently occurred when they got caught in the fearsome gin-traps, which also proliferated. It was accepted that those who set traps should check them twice a day but this did not always happen.

Approaching the unmoving rabbit, which was just across a hollow, they all stopped, fascinated with their discovery. A stoat was watching it from a few yards away and the rabbit, mesmerised, sat stock-still. The stoat, quite a lot smaller than its prey, seemed too intent to notice the presence of the boys. Then, with a lightning dart it was upon it and with the briefest of squeals the rabbit was dead. Rushing forward, the boys scared the stoat away and inspected the rabbit. Just a small wound, administered in seconds, to the nape of its neck was all that could be seen.

"We'll take that un as well," said George.

Leaving the field by the bottom gate they were suddenly shocked to see the body of a man lying near the roadside. Stunned into silence, they prepared to run off, but the ever-inquisitive George edged warily around to look at the face, which was nestled into the soft grass.

Smiling, but in a hushed tone he said, "It's alright, it's only Tammy Bishop, a sleeping it off."

"Tammy", Fred Bishop, lived on his own in a tiny cottage, now part of No. 74. He was a first-class worker for most of the time but on occasion he would take a week or two off and go on a real bender. His present plight was quite common during these sessions. The rest of the year he left alcohol alone. This time he was on the bank, but sometimes he collapsed on the side of the road itself.

Recovering from this experience, they pressed on past the first house where Francis Witchell could be seen practising his tree climbing, his mother dragging him out of the large apple tree. His father, Alf, in charge of several council lengthmen, the invaluable workmen whose responsibility it was to keep their own village and local roads neat and tidy, was busy whetting a scythe ready for work on Tuesday. The broad, shining blade sang as it was stroked with the round whetstone, kept moist by regular sprays of well directed spittle and would be as sharp as a razor. When it became dulled it would be continually "touched up" again during the days work.

Alf's brother, a retired policeman, lived at Hillside, farther down on the right. Two other brothers lived at Windrush. Harry, next to The Vicarage and Archie, an electrician, with his sister, where Honour Balfour of the old political family now lives. Despite his calling and the fact that his rent was only half a crown a week, Archie refused to make his life any easier by adding any more electrical fittings to his house. "I ain't spending nothing on somebody else's property!"

Big Jim Smith, retired now from his blacksmiths shop across the green, stood by his gate at the thatched cottage. His son, Harry, dubbed "peg-leg" by the boys, now lived in the house by the disused smithy. He'd lost his leg serving the country in The Great War, but managed very well with his wooden one. Jim and his son both had powerful voices and could converse across the green without leaving their front doors.

Harry and his son, Tom, were sunning themselves, sitting in the generous stone porch-way or entrance to the house. Tom, nicknamed "Leggit", was one of the fastest boys on two legs and acquired his name from the old words of encouragement shouted to someone obviously in a hurry, "Leg it you!"

The Green, the irregular, grassy area, which is central to the village of Little Barrington, is reputed to have been a quarry. What better way than to build the village houses from the stone, there on site?

Well worn paths radiated across the Green, consolidated by the heavy tread of generations of cottagers as they fetched their water from the sparkling spring, whilst wisps of smoke seeped out of the ever smouldering heaps of ash and rubbish piled down the bank in front of the houses on the west side.

Over on that side, behind the village pump, Miss Woods, the schoolmistress and her neighbour, Miss Kirby, could be seen chatting in front of their cottages, the one on the left still having its old thatched roof. Jim could little foresee that in some twenty seven years time he would be lucky enough to buy them both and convert them into his own house; the thatch would be fallen in and Miss Woods passed on – all for the princely sum of eleven hundred and fourteen hundred pounds respectively.

Further down, Frank Dunford, a tall, strong, young man was sitting on the stone doorstep, whittling away, making a new haft for his felling axe. He and Ted Lord were guilty of felling thousands of trees in the neighbourhood. After chopping out huge wedges from the base with their razor-sharp felling axes, they could, using a long, narrow, cross-cut saw, fell trees to any point of the compass as accurately and nearly as quickly as can the present forester with his modern aids. The "chips", those first wedgy bits, and all the small branches and brushwood were soon collected for cottagers' fires, after the main timber had been cut and transported away by Groves, the timber-merchants, of Milton-under-Wychwood.

"I wish as Haywards' shop was open, I couldn't half do with a sherbet dab", complained John.

"Lots of kids pinches a jumbo when the old girls got her back turned."

Little Barrington. Originally two cottages (converted in 1964)
l/h Miss Kirby   r/h Miss A. S. Woods

All types of sweets were dubbed jumbos even though the name really applied to the gob-stopper size. Haywards shop, a typical village store, sold everything from bars of salt to paraffin, cheese to pickling vinegar, ising glass for preserving eggs to postcards. The sepia-coloured penny postcards were over produced by Raphael Tuck and Sons and Frank Packer of Chipping Norton, so that they were never updated and continued from year to year. Their quality was good and many hundreds still survive. Mrs. Hayward ran the shop with some assistance from daughter Alice, while her husband, Edward, was the local jobbing builder. He was helped by his son Arthur, whose delightfully carved miniature stone boots and sundry ornaments still abound in the village.

"They says as the shop had used to be a pub, it was supposed to be called The Black Dog. There was the cellar at the back where they keeps the paraffin and the shop was the bar and the snug was on the other side of the passage," reflected Cyril. "What's a snug, sounds like something to do with smugglers?" asked Jim who, like the others really knew nothing about pubs.

"Well it's a little room, that's all I knows," said Cyril.

All the pubs were blessed with a snug room, a warm and intimate retreat for the favoured few. A congenial meeting room, a place of secrets, a venue for illicit card games and an after hours drinking haven.

Just at this moment a small, scruffy figure, with an untidy beard, came shuffling round from the back of the house. One hand clutched a lumpy paper bag and from the other swung a small, fire-blackened pot on its thin wire handle.

"There's Happy Jack, just bin round and got some tea and grub from Mrs. Hayward. 'Ee's always coming to our door a begging, our mum don't let 'im in cos er says as ee hums too much."

To hum had nothing to do with music, but was the colloquial expression for something giving off a bad smell.

"Ee'll be 'ere all summer again. Our dad says ee's got back in the Lime Kiln", said John.

The Lime Kiln was a small hut built in a land depression on the right of the Rissington road. Mortar for bonding the stone houses was made from a lime mix. It was achieved by heating limestone to a powder and had been produced there for centuries. Happy Jack turned up every summer and became part of the community. He always seemed happy and won certain affection from the many households he visited. A knock on the back door would often reveal his familiar face, right hand extended with his horrid black pot waiting to be filled. Many were those who could ill afford the tea which they made for him or the couple of scones that he was usually given. The door was shut in his face while the tea was made from the ever-simmering kettle on the old black grate and when it was handed out to him, he was always grateful and wet off "humming" and whistling at the same time.

Often other tramps worked their way through the villages and seemed always to know on which door to knock. It was generally believed that the fraternity always left a secret sign on the premises, so that those following could easily find the homes of the soft-hearted. Mrs. Hayward was certainly one with a heart of gold.

The tall figure of an elderly man was just going into his garden at the far end of the next row of cottages. A quiet man who was dressed in a brown suit, unlike the black and dark grey of most of the locals and wore a floppy fedora hat.

"There's old Louis Organ just gone in, our dad says 'ee's a Communist and that means 'ee's a spy." volunteered George.

"Perhaps he's been to talk to that White Russian your dad's got up at the garage." Louis was a very skilled shoemaker and repairer and pursued his trade in a well-equipped shed at the top of his garden. He always seemed a lonely and secretive man, giving rise to certain doubts about his twilight activities. A visit to his workshop with its big glass windows was a rare experience.

"No it was probably his bosses that chucked Mathew Sokolov out", said Jim, who had heard about the Russian revolution.

"See that big archway in the middle of that row of houses? They say that years ago it went right through and there was a path from here right up to the church."

It was now blocked part way, but formed a very generous porch.

"And Stratford's house, that's supposed to be the oldest house around here. It's in the Doomsday Book and that's ever so old."

Amongst all the low-ceilinged, low door-framed cottages which must have been built for a much shorter generation of inhabitants, and which have since caused so many cracked skulls, Stratford's house, with its sun-dial on it must be the oldest. Its denizens would have been little more than midgets; who else would want such little headspace?

Trooping out of Little Barrington, they were hailed by Frank Jones, who, with his wife was tending the garden in the last house on the left.

"Hi boys, where dids't thee catch they?" referring to the rabbits which were now beginning to attract the attention of a number of blow flies.

"Well even if thee dids't catch em in Quarry Banks don't let old Jennings see thee. Any road, thee oughtn't to be catching they on a Sunday."

Mrs. Jones, the last village woman still wearing button-up boots and always a straw bonnet, very prim and proper, looked on with great distaste and urged them to throw them over the hedge.

In the days before refrigeration, blowflies laying their eggs in any meat product could soon turn it into a seething mass of white maggots. Even the local butcher had problems and had to rely on fly screens. Every cottage had its larder and its meat safe whose door was screened by a fly proof wire mesh. For those lucky enough to be able to patronise the butcher, it came as second nature to wash and inspect the meat before consigning it to the well-scrubbed safe. The local butcher was Bill Pitts from Windrush who delivered his orders in a pony and trap, and it has to be acknowledged that Bill's idea of hygiene left much to be desired. Surprisingly, in spite of the modern proliferation of highly paid food inspectors, who monitor the ever-increasing burden of our own and EC directives, no one seemed to suffer any ill effects. After all, when we get "back to basics", the lives of Aborigines and others are sustained by eating larvae. Apart from the self-evident fact that all red meat is so well cooked that whatever it is host to must surely perish.

Rejecting this advice, "No, we be going to kip 'em", they strode on towards The Fox. The two branches of the Windrush were on their right and keeper Jennings could be seen in his garden in front of the house across the valley. A big heron stood motionless in the water and as they watched it speared a trout, dextrously adjusted it in its beak and swallowed it whole.

"How does they eat 'em like that? I don't like fish 'cos of all they bones," said Sidney.

It was mutually agreed that they must spit them up again.

Reaching The Fox orchard, which was a prime target in apple scragging time, John volunteered,

"They tadpoles eats each other. I 'ad a big jar full and when I'd 'ad em a couple of weeks they grew some legs and then ate each other."

The orchard contained a semi-circle of stagnant water, a bend of the main river, which had been left when the squire had paid men to dig through the neck of an ox-bow and so straightened the course. The main river now flowed happily through this breach and the ox-bow was left as a quiet haven for teeming aquatic life. Each spring the surface was covered with frogspawn and the budding boy naturalists scooped it out into jars, which were stood on the kitchen window sills.

Before the algae turned the glass green and opaque the metamorphous of the frogs could be observed. First the frantic agitation of the dark spotted jelly, then the round tailed tadpole and lastly the tadpole with developing legs. The cycle was never completed, no frogs ever developed to the point of jumping out. They couldn't, the glass was too high and too slick, but more importantly it was never appreciated that the specimens needed more than a change of water to survive and so they turned cannibal, the last one dying from starvation.

Whilst being strategically situated at the confluence of three roads, each leading to the different villages of Great and Little Barrington and Windrush, The Fox Inn is also on the River Windrush. From a wharf here the local building stone for St. Pauls was floated down to London. A long and hazardous journey!

The window shutters were well secured, it being Sunday; they would stay that way until the morrow.

"I'll bet old Frankie Paintin's busy a writing 'is poetry,'" suggested John. "'Ave you ever sin any on it? It's some poor old tack."

In fact Frank was very proud of his poems, had them properly printed and some of the originals still survive and have improved for the keeping.

The Fox Inn

I have copied this one from an original in my possession.

A DAY AT THE FOX INN, BARRINGTON

In Cotswolds sweet vale, by the side of a brook,
Stands an old-fashioned inn in a quiet shady nook,
Protected from winter's wild fusillade
By woods which in summer afford pleasant shade,
An inn you may enter where you will be sure
Of a welcome as soon as you enter the door.
On entering the inn you make for the bar;
The landlord will care for and garage your car.
You order a lunch which is quickly prepared.
You've no need to ask if the beds are well aired.
Then enjoying your lunch you call for the bill,
Which you promptly settle with downright good will.
For you find the fare ample, the tariff is light,
So you quickly decide you'll remain for the night.
Then strolling around you're inclined for a wander
Through byways and fields to the mill over yonder.
Passing the mill over footbridge and stile,
You linger to gaze in the stream for a while.
Watching the fishes sporting about,
Roach, dace and grayling and bright speckled trout.
Then crossing the meadow to old Minnow Lane
Which you find leads you back to the old inn again.
At the end of the lane, pause, take in the scene,
Spreading before you, peaceful, serene.
An old Cotswold village set in a glade,
Old houses, quaint doorways with seats in the shade.
While down at your feet spreads broad open green,
And meandering through it cool sparkling stream;
The rooks cawing loudly in tall elms nearby.
And a lark gaily warbling its way to the sky,
Adds harmonious touch to this memorable scene
Of beauty spots surely of Cotswold's the queen.
Then the sun slowly sinking away in the west,
You will be thinking of supper and rest,
Slowly back your way to the inn you will wend,
For days e'en as this much come to an end.
Then supper and chat you call for your light,
Wishing both host and hostess a cheery good-night.

"Hi Jack, what hast thee bin at? A fishing I'll warrant." shouted George to two boys who were clambering over the stone stile just before the bridge.

"Did'st thee catch owt?"

It was fairly evident that Jack Dadge and Bert Phipps were concealing something wrapped in a large dock leaf and that their pockets were bulging. Being reluctant to share any information they made off up the tree-lined path to the Windrush road. They'd obviously had some sport fishing off The Fox bridge. Hand lines trawled down the current would often produce a useful fish, while the young sportsman concealed his line bobbin as he turned, with overdone innocence, to nod to passers by.

Jack's father, Fred Dadge, was the organist for Windrush church. Both Jack and Bert were later to join the wavy navy during the impending war. With a name like Albert Mariner Phipps, Bert's future seemed predestined. It was quite amazing how many youths from the area, which could hardly be further from the sea, did join the Navy.

Now along the causeway between the two stone bridges. These bridges, built many years ago, with their beautifully executed stone arches still survive the immense weight of modern, heavy transport and yet at the time of their construction nothing heavier than the stresses caused by stone carts and timber wagons could possibly have been foreseen. Strongs Causeway, named after its builders, that same family of master masons who had played such a part in the building of St. Paul's Cathedral. In times of extreme flooding the water does lap onto it, but ever since, it has provided a solid thoroughfare between the villages. The big wall to one side provided privacy for the big house, but the other affords an open vista down the valley, dominated by Little Barrington Grove.

"I be a going along the wall," said John and, followed by the others, scrambled up and evading the several overhanging branches, traversed the Causeway from on high, all being prepared to make a quick descent should their folly be threatened by the advent of chiding elders or owners. It was then a perfectly straight parapet but is now a bit wavy after the toppers were reset. The blade of a World War Two, American forces, Caterpillar D8 bulldozer, loaded on a heavy transporter, dislodged several yards of the top courses and the latter day repairers failed to equal the perfection of the original builders.

From the next river bridge the damage to the banks and riverbed, caused by a recent operation, was still terribly obvious. Because of the silting up of this man-made stretch the whole half-mile or so had been emptied by damming up the feeder weir and allowing all the water to pass down the old natural course. This resulted in rapidly diminishing pools, alive with desperate fish and eels, which were quickly harvested or allowed to die. When ready, a steam engine, operating a drag-line and bucket, dug and scooped out the deposits as well as the bed of the river. Hundreds of tons of dark, evil-smelling mud was thus deposited on the south bank. The riverbed was destroyed and the bank became mis-shaped. Ecologically, this feat of engineering was a disaster. Years were to pass before the river settled and because of its extra width and scooped bank, it was certainly going to silt up more quickly than before.

Daring also to walk this bridge parapet, they jumped down at the other side and ran over to the "Cold Bath". This spring, unfailing through even the most severe of droughts, gushed from the base of a wall and flowed into two in line stone troughs, the top one for the use of mankind and the bottom one for the horses to slake their thirst. Then by way of a sunken pipe it joined a small channel leading to the river. This channel, fed from one arch of the road bridge, carried the water to operate a water ram. This ram in turn pumped the fresh spring water up to the village reservoir. The reservoir water was then piped to certain farms and village houses. Some of the pipes were buried too shallow and when the weather was particularly cold they froze.

As a result, Jim, amongst others, had to journey right down to the spring for household needs. This usually happened when there was snow on the ground and little wooden sledges with buckets were the easiest and most interesting way of performing this heavy task. It goes without saying that even if the buckets didn't fall off, quite half of the contents slopped away during transit.

"I fell in here, too, when I was young," said Jim.

Always the rebel, George said, "Come on you lot, let's try and get into the Summer House."

With extreme trepidation the others followed him. Over the wall opposite and down the Jacob's Ladder used by the gamekeepers and into the bushes bordering the expanse of lawned pleasure gardens.

"Keep quiet and follow I," was the unnecessary order.

After creeping up through the bushes until the goal came between them, and the likely presence of the squire or his family, they cautiously broke cover and sped into the building.

The Summer House is a circular, stone pilastered building with a domed roof, not unlike a small version of the pigeon house, built to one side of the lawns and affording a shaded and uninterrupted view of the Broadwater, the valley and the mixed woodlands.

Having achieved their goal, something to boast about, they spent scant time there and quickly returned to the road.

Only the hill to ascend now to get back home. It is by way of being a cutting flanked by high, tree-grown banks on one side, but dominated by an immense stone wall on the other. The shrubby ground behind the first, low, left-hand wall rises sharply to a hidden, levelled area, which forms the kitchen gardens for the big house. As a gruesome point of interest it may be worth recording that years later, a bunch of cattle which had escaped and found their way to the lower reaches, were panicked into heading uphill behind the wall and, finding themselves trapped in the apex of the wedge-shaped enclosure, were propelled by sheer weight of numbers, over the parapet and fell, with disastrous consequences onto the road far below. A very messy, bloody and chilling scene.

Dark haired Peggy Sollis watched her schoolboy friends go by from behind a wicket gate half way up the hill. She, like Gerard Lobb lived in a pair of cottages screened from the road but with their own superb views across the valley.

The pair of houses near the top of the hill were homes to Fred Sweet, the head gardener and the Tuffnell family. Betty Tuffnell, a proper tomboy, who delighted in climbing trees but was shy, nevertheless gave a languid wave.

Henry, her father, was footman valet and her mother, the housekeeper in the big house.

Jim was once invited to go to the housekeeper's room, the family being away and shown around the house. The long, dark passages, the rows of bells hanging muted under ivory name plates; The Blue Room, the Drawing Room, Lady Talbot's room, which, agitated by means of wires and pulleys, summoned the servants to execute the family's slightest whim. The front hall dominated by a huge stuffed bear, and inside the back door, remarkably, an electric service lift.

Tea and delicate sandwiches were served in front of a generous fireplace, amidst an aura of authority and respectability.

The electricity for the lift and general lighting was supplied by a very large electric light plant housed in the top floor of the stable block which backs onto the graveyard. It was immaculately tended by George Herbert the head chauffeur, helped by his under chauffeur, Dick Messer, and was started by firing a cartridge into the cylinder. The resultant explosion kicked it into life. The fifty two, big glass, two volt, lead cell batteries, some thirty inches high by fifteen inches square and collectively containing many gallons of acid, produced a 100 watt DC (Direct Current.) The plant was eventually broken up and sold to a scrap man. The weight of lead was enormous, the brass fittings, bearings etc from the engine, though beautifully cast, were reduced to scrap.

The dairy in the top right hand corner was supplied by Daniel Lobb's Guernseys. The milk was transported down in an iron-wheeled milk churn. After the big house had been supplied the rest was "separated" for cream and for butter making. The cream was put into a wooden butter churn and laboriously rotated until the butter was made. The skimmed milk was then carried in pails on a yoke up to the village. Here, in the building by the War Memorial, where a door gave access to a "weighing room", and which, when opened provided a serving hatch, it was sold for a halfpenny a pint. This work was usually done by Joss Sollis, Colin's father or by Connie Woodley, later

Mr Michael Mallard near
War Memorial, village pump and
weigh bridge behind

Robin Leach's mother. The metal weighbridge used for weighing carts, empty and loaded, was controlled and measured by a long weighing beam inside the room. Weights were pushed and pulled along the beam until the balance was found and the weight recorded.

Beyond the big, wrought iron gates of the drive down to the house, another high wall continued, breached by a door which served as entrance both to Michael Mallard's house and the Reading Room. Michael was the under coachman whose job, like that of his old boss, was now redundant. One of his daughters later married the Vicar, the Reverend Gerald Parkinson. At that time The Vicarage was in Taynton and he served the three parishes of Great and Little Barrington with Taynton.

In the dark evenings and winter nights the doorway and the steep steps inside were illuminated by a large oil lantern sited on top of the wall. The glassless framework survives today!

Michael looked after the Reading Room, a separate purpose-built building next to his house.

"Has't thee ever been in the Reading Room? My dad goes down, but we boys ain't allowed."

"What's it like in there?" asked Cyril.

Jim knew because his grandfather was largely in charge of it and he was sometimes allowed in, on pain of dire consequences should he break the silence.

A fire at one end, flanked by bookshelves, good Windsor chairs at either side and a small reading table for the current newspaper, The London Illustrated Evening News and a copy of Punch magazine. The village elders sat quietly reading, smoking their pipes and conversing in restrained tones. The cosy atmosphere thus created a welcome respite from the rigours of the outside world. In the winter, with the heavy curtains drawn against the outside elements, the heat from the fire, the pleasant odour of tobacco smoke and the fumes from the oil lamps produced a soporific effect. Grey heads drooped and nodded as their owners savoured the haven so far removed from their harsh world.

The big oil lamp with its reflectors, shed light on a three-quarter-size billiard table in the centre of the room. The young men playing communicated in hushed tones and the only audible sounds were those of the click of the cues and balls and the rattle of the scoreboard.

Just up the roadside path two men, George Berry and Caleb Stratford, had stopped to watch an aeroplane flying overhead. George had probably been down to the big house to replenish the fuel supply.

The buildings near to the servants entrance, the back door, were stacked with tons of coal and coke and mountains of wood blocks. Daily, barrowloads of fuel were needed to fire the boilers, from which miles of big old iron pipe carried the hot water needed to service and warm this mini community. Also to feed the fires in the family rooms, as well as those for the housekeeper and other important members of the retinue.

The blocks were sawn from estate wood in the wood-yard adjoining Mike Mallard's house. Here a steam traction engine powered a circular saw-bench used for rough work. Sometimes when planks and other building materials were required, Jack Berry, the driver, drove it over to the estate yard in the village. There the carpenters' shop was situated and there a sawpit enabled huge trunks to be converted into fine lengths of timber, gateposts and fencing rail. With smoke belching from its tall stack, the engine was a formidable sight for small boys. Although it worked amongst wood, the sparks from the funnel and the firebox never caused any major problem.

Jack was once hauled in front of Northleach Magistrates Court accused of exceeding the 6mph speed limit for that vehicle!

The same could hardly be said about the steam threshing engine, which had come to the adjacent Park Farm. Set up in the rick-yard to thresh the wheat and barley ricks huddled together there, a wayward spark had ignited one rick causing a chain reaction. The resulting devastation was far too much for Burford fire brigade to deal with, using the antiquated pump which they had brought with them. A terrifying sight when viewed from Jim's bedroom, a bare hundred yards away. All was lost and farmer Charles Bartlett was a poorer man.

Caleb was in Sunday best; complete with black polished leggings. He'd doubtless been down to his beloved church, possibly to wind the church clock set high in the belfry tower. Winding it was a regular task and involved climbing the stone steps, a feat which became ever more hazardous as the years took their toll on the dedicated verger. Villagers' clocks and watches were checked and reset to the quarter, half-hourly and hourly strikes and chimes of his church timepiece.

Caleb was also a darts player and it was an education to listen to him score. In his deep voice he intoned, "twenty seven, Abide with Me, sixty one, Christians Awake, or ninety nine Ride On, ride on in Majesty", being able to relate the hymnal to the score. This accomplishment was always overshadowed by the cry "Lord Sherbun", which heralded the score of thirty three, AD33, being the noble Lord Sherborne's universally recognised car registration number.

Stopping by these two elders, the boys also watched the big De Havilland bi-plane, which had probably taken off from the repairers at Witney, and listened to the conversation,

"By Guy ain't 'ee up a depth, Ow would'st thee like to be up there with 'ee then George?" asked Caleb.

"I ouldn't mind, as long as I could a kip one foot on the ground," replied George. Enthralled with this snippet of conversation the boys, standing at a respectful distance as they continued to watch the slow progress of the aircraft, were treated to a further gem which followed Caleb's question, "'ow's thy missus George?"

"Er's alright, but you knows women, suspicious creatures they be. 'Er always have a been. Dost thee know as we 'and't a bin married no time and I wanted a bit of muck for my garden, so I'm a walking up the street with Bob, that's my old sheepdog as was and I meets Farmer Bartlett. I says, Hast thee got any muck as I can 'ave for my garden?"

"Yes George 'ee says."

"Then 'e looks down at old Bob and 'ee says,

"George, thy dog ain't a got a collar on, hast thee got a licence for 'im?"

"Yes", I says.

"How much be they now?" he says.

"Seven an sixpence a year", says I. "I pays three and ninepence a yer for 'ee. Ow's that?" 'ee says.

"Well if theest look at that old dog 'ee 'ave got two yers". (ears)

"Didn't like it a lot, but then 'ee says, muck George, course thee can 'ave some muck, there's a pile on it up by the bowsen, thee can 'ave as much as thee'd a mind to get."

"So I does no more but goes 'ome and fetches my barrow and four grain and gets up there. And there was a good heap on it, just what I'd a wanted. So I starts muddling away at it, but dost thee know, that old bugger 'ee 'adnt told I as his little Jersey bull was up there and that little devil came up behind me, 'it me up the ass as clean as a whistle and cut I into a pile of straw rubbish as was there, as sweet as a nut. Any road, when I gets 'ome, I'd still got a bit of straw stuck in me hair and me jumper and my missus says to I, 'er says,

"What hast thee bin up to?"

"So I told 'er, but 'er says to I, 'er says, T'aint a bull as 'ad thee, 'er says, It' thee as has been bulling". "Er always was suspicious".

Savouring this gem of conversation, the boys left. Jim, the youngest, enquiring as to its obvious significance, because some of the others were having trouble containing their mirth,

"What did he mean, a bulling?" said he.

Ignoring the difficult question, George said,

"Come on then, let's get home, I can do with my tea. It's Sunday and we has butter today".

Butter would be a treat in many households where bread and lard or bread and scrat-on would be the norm. "Bread and scrat-on" was bread with butter scratched on to it and then "scrat off" again, leaving only a hint of butter.

Jim, somewhat privileged, had butter everyday but within strict rules. First, a slice of bread and butter, a second slice with paste or Marmite added but if he wanted jam there must be no butter. Another quotation from his father, "My father never let us have butter with jam and nor can you". Without butter the bread gets jam-soaked and soggy.

Sometimes he would help butter making in the dairy that was attached to the back of Park Farm House. Mrs. Bartlett, the farmer's wife, would even allow him to finish the pats off by rolling a wooden roller across the top of them, so as to leave a decoration of nuts and leaves indented into them; a wonderfully satisfying job.

John appeared to be engrossed with something he'd just picked up, prompting Cyril to ask what it was.

"Come on, let's have a look".

"No, it's mine and I'm keeping it, I dunno what it is yet".

"Well come on let's see".

"No, you wunt know either".

"Perhaps I wunt, but our dad always says as two yeads be better nur one even if they be sheeps heads.

"I know what it is, our dad's got one of they in his tractor. It's a dipstick for checking the oil in the engine with".

John's father, Tom Clements, working for Mr.Bartlett on Park Farm, drove the first Fordson tractor there and it was ominously predicted that the fumes from the short exhaust pipe blowing back into the unprotected face of the driver would soon kill him. Not only was he assailed by these vapours belching from the engine, but also by all the elements, winter and summer, that nature could throw at him. The engine ran on T.V.O. (Tractor vaporising oil), but was started with petrol, that warmed up the vaporiser, which was part of the exhaust manifold system.

Tractor cabs were luxuries of the future and developed from a crude box structure to the present day comforts of heating, radio and the ubiquitous mobile phone. The shaking he got when driving it on firm surfaces, as the large metal "spuds" on the iron wheels lumbered along, could hardly have helped either.

"It's probably George Hall's, forgot to put it back in, we'll take it back down there anyway."

When they got back up to the War Memorial the usual knot of old men was grouped around the village pump nearby. It was an obvious meeting place. A short wall behind it enclosing a small area in which grew a few straggly bushes and a laburnum tree. Harry Bedwell, Jim Sollis, the patriarch of such a large village family, and Bill Cyphus were enjoying the sun. Harry Bedwell, resplendent in his straw hat was moving a length of straw around his mouth, as he complained yet again about the pump.

"Keeps telling Harry Barnes about it. Has to bring near a half a bucket of water to prime it just to get one back out".

This meant that the leather washer on the pump plunger had worn. It was only by means of removing the top of the cast iron pump and pouring in a quantity of water to prime it, that sufficient suction could be induced to raise the water up to the spout. It was always nice to arrive while someone else was there and to find that it was already working well.

Poor Billie Bedwell was sitting quietly nearby in his wickerwork Bath chair. Jim always wondered why he was an invalid and it was only at his early death that he was told that Billie had contracted a nasty and incurable disease whilst serving in the war.

Splitting up at the top of the village the group headed homewards. They'd see each other after tea. This Sunday there had been Holy Communion at 8 a.m. and Matins at 11o'clock. Last week it had been 10 a.m. Matins and 6 p.m. Evensong.

For Jim, as always, traditional Sunday teatime enhanced by peaches and cream.

Milk and cream, delivered to the door by Mark Cook who lived near to Barrington Farm where he worked for the farmer Mr. Browning. He arrived in good time with a couple of pails of fresh, richly creamed milk either end of his yoke and filled the milk jugs by scooping it out with a long-handled ladle. He had a wonderful way of predicting the weather, "Going to be a nice day today missus. The thrush is right at the top of the tree and singing her heart out." Other weather was accurately predicted by how far up or down the songbird sat.

The dark nights, when Grandfather, in dark grey suit and light grey woollen smoking waistcoat, would retire to the drawing room to read from his formidable library, were now over. Shakespeare, Dickens and H.G. Wells were shelved among massive tomes of knowledge and beautiful, leather-bound, gold-edged books, received as honour prizes by both him and his wife from the Diocesan Board of Education. They had both schooled at Abingdon and he had then gone on to Culham College. The house was the old village vicarage and he seemed at peace within it. Gone were the servants of yesteryear, but, still there, the elaborate bell-pulls either side of the fire-place and the bells in the outside passage which had summoned them.

It was pleasant to take an early evening walk, dressed in Sunday clothes, short trousered suit, collar and tie. The collar was always starched and held in place by front and back collar studs. These were always getting mislaid. Long stud, with a spring top at the front and a short plain stud for the back. So many anguished shouts of, "I can't find my back stud", echoed through houses where the men, usually collarless, were struggling to fit starched collars round tanned necks.

Great Barrington War Memorial
rear of Post Office behind

War Memorial from Jim's bedroom
window

CHAPTER SIX

The usual knot of boys was waiting by the War Memorial, which, with its low stone wall, was accepted as the focal point for such gatherings. Jim Adams was just letting himself out of the estate yard, whose joinery shop, accommodating four or five workbenches, fronted the yard. Also there were building materials necessary for the general upkeep of the estate property. The stone roofing slates required by Sid Mills and Dick Sollis, the fencing and railing posts, the bags of cement and lime. Outside the carpenter's shop stood two big grindstones for tool sharpening. They each consisted of a large stone wheel as big as a mill wheel, revolved by a generous handle and suspended upright in a low wooden trough, which, lead-sealed, held the water which lubricated or whetted the outside edge of the stone as it revolved. It was, necessarily, a slow turn on the wheel. Any undue speed generated by an enthusiastic boy would send a fine spray of sandy coloured water over the hapless individual who was holding the tool against the stone. Jim had learnt this lesson well after being chided by his grandfather who sometimes went there to put an edge on his kindling axe.

At the bottom of the yard was a large sawpit. It had probably been there since the days when "saw-pit" really meant what it said. Before circular saws the pit was used so that one man could stand above the timber which was being reduced, whilst the other was down in the pit. A long crosscut saw could then be pushed and pulled in a near vertical manner. The poor chap in the pit, though only having a downward pull was working in a shower of sawdust. The sweatier he got the more the sawdust stuck to him.

It was now dominated by a long saw bench and circular saw. The pit became a receptacle for the sawdust which was emptied and burnt off when filled. The power was supplied by Jack Berry's steam traction engine. This fiery, hissing monster made short work of even the biggest rounds of timber.

These great tree trunks had been carried here by the couple of timber carriages which stood nearby. Theirs was the heaviest job on the estate. Standing on four big, wooden, steel-rimmed wheels they were essentially two axles joined by a long pole which could be extended or contracted to suit the length of the timber. The shafts at the front end were designed to take four of the strongest shire horses. Two poles at either end were shaped in a big upright vee. To load the timber, one side of the vee at each end was removed after positioning the carriage alongside the log. Then poles to act as ramps were located, chains or ropes were secured to the carriage, passed under the timber, fed back over the carriage and secured to special traces on the horses which had been un-harnessed from the shafts. With two chains, two struggling horses and plenty of encouragement from the drivers, the log was rolled up to lodge against the front and back vee poles until the other poles were inserted, thereby securing it in the top of the two crucifixes. This done, the horses re-harnessed, it only remained to drag it out of the wood. This was a Herculean task. The narrow wheels sank into the soft ground; the shires hooves churned up the firmest of terrain and the men used long poles as levers to help. Even the rutted farm roads were unused to such treatment and crumbled at the edges. When the village road was reached the whole moved well but going downhill then became hazardous. Such weight required braking, which was accomplished with iron shoes or drags dropped in front of the wheels, which skidded rather than turned, wooden brake blocks applied to the outer rim and even help from poles levered against them.

There wasn't too much to do on a summer Sunday evening. Familiar courting couples took their evening stroll up the Rissington road. Ray Herbert and Mae, Roland Preston and Elsie. George

Herbert cycled past to check his electric light plant and Joss Sollis came from the buildings after milking the cows.

The boys sauntered off down the village. These light evenings were nice but not exciting like the dark, winter nights. Then, the community shut indoors, curtains drawn, was the time for eerie and frightening games of hide and seek. The dark alleys, garden walls and clumps of shrubbery allowed both predator and prey an advantage. Even the darkest night gave dim silhouettes of familiar and intimate landmarks and the children, boys and girls, could chase each other with utmost confidence and in absolute safety.

Front door knockers could be banged with impunity, the outside darkness making it impossible for the owner, staring from a lighted room, to see the culprits. On occasion and after prolonged attention the man of the house would react, swing a bright flashlight and if able to catch someone would administer some summary justice. This was painfully received but accepted as par for the course and never reported at home for fear of more verbal and physical chastisement.

Shepherd Russell was working in his garden, helped by his son, Fred, and watched by his wife and daughter, Doris. Fred became a great gardener with a glorious show of flowers, prize onions and football-sized cabbages. He used a long-handled four grain-pitch fork to dig in copious amounts of pig muck from the sties at the top of the garden. Yet his unforgettable remark would be,

"My garden's so poor as it won't even grow weeds."

Doris was later to marry Jack Pitts, the butcher's son.

Joe Leach was down by his bake-house, watching his son Peter wheeling fuel ready for the next days baking. It would be a very early start, long before dawn so that the loaves, seed cakes and lard cakes would be fresh and ready in good time.

The door on "The Stores" was closed but someone, probably Kathy Hall, would be in there manning the telephone exchange. Word had got around that Mrs. Forrest, the matriarch of the fair-ground family had been there the day before complaining of a cold. "I'll have a bottle of Owbridges Lung Tonic", she said, and despite the printed warnings had upended it there and then and drunk it all in one go. Hopefully it helped, obviously it hadn't been lethal.

Now, past the old prison it was time to be on best behaviour as they approached "The Hollies" where the headmaster was flicking a yellow duster over his shiny Austin Seven. His wife, Jude, as he called her, subdued the lads with a frosty look. She was the head of Taynton School and it was gratefully acknowledged that the children there underwent an even more rigid discipline than did those at Barrington.

The Smithy with its stable type door stood quiet, but beyond, outside the two houses which have now been demolished, Irene, Shepherd Preston's daughter and Margaret Cambray were playing. After subdued greetings they then passed Caleb Stratford's house, where his daughter was standing behind the garden gate, Kathy, a grown woman, was very "simple minded" and a dreadful problem for her mother who, consumed with arthritis, received no help from a non-existent welfare state.

Barrington Forge. Bill Hall and son Brian
Smithy now closed

In the next garden, Dennis, a well liked youth, one of the sons of the large Cole family was working. He was later to lose his life after the W.W.II D-Day landings having previously escaped from Dunkirk in 1940. A very sad loss for the whole of the community. At the last gate stood 'Granny Barnes'. Behind her was the small cottage, which was knocked down after she moved with Leonard, her son, to another house at the top of the lane opposite the Smithy that in turn was later demolished.

Rounding the bottom of the village they circled the big, stone hay-barn. The heavy wooden doors were propped open to give light to a pen of young calves. One of these doors was later to fall on Kathy Hall causing serious injury from which accident she was lucky to survive.

Up the back lane, Granny Clements, sunning herself in the garden on the right, past Harry Barnes' house and the estate office where Mr. Radway, the agent held sway, to the Village Hall which had been built in a part of the playground field where the fair now stood.

"Wish as they'd still have the big tent", said George.

Indeed the fair seemed smaller and to have lost its focal point. Until the Village Hall was built the Club Dinner was held in a seemingly vast marquee around which the amusements could centre. Its erection was of riveting interest. The area where it stood had to be cleared of the seasons cowpats and horse droppings. When erected and furnished with long, wooden trestle tables and forms to sit on, it acquired its own secretive and strange atmosphere. This delighted the boys who slid surreptitiously under its canvas walls to savour the heady environment.

"Got to get home now", said Jim and thrilled with anticipation of his visit to the fair tomorrow he made his way home, past Jim Sollis' pig-sties which were now still quiet, empty and with doors ajar.

Back at the house, mother enjoying the late evening sun, checking and tending her beloved garden, grandfather reading, sister already abed, there was only time to have a cup of cocoa and retire himself. It was difficult to immerse himself in one of the books there: The Scarlet Pimpernel or The Last of the Mohicans were far better appreciated when the nights were dark. After lights out they could be read in the steamy atmosphere created by withdrawing under the bedclothes and reading by torchlight. The sounds of the other children still playing outside were not conducive to full concentration.

The new day dawned, soon father could be heard leaving in the old Austin 12 and Jim could get up for the big day.

A token wash under the cold tap at the scullery sink was followed by a quick rub at his teeth with a toothbrush that was a little more than freshened by scrubbing it into a tin of Gibbs Dentifrice. Toothpaste in tubes had so far eluded the village, if indeed there was then such a product. Whilst spitting it into the sink he noticed that father had shaved this morning. Thick, grey splodges of shaving soap, tinged with red, bore witness that the cut-throat razor had caused a nick or two and, that like most men, he would be sporting a little tuft of cotton wool on his top lip or on his cheek. The thick, leather razor strop hung on the wall, secured by a strong hook so that it could be stretched tight whilst the stropping was in progress.

Grandfather seemed particularly chirpy this morning, as well he should. This day would mark his Benefit Society's Jubilee. Some had thought it better to drop it this year because it was so close to the coronation of King George VI and his queen, but were quite properly silenced. The sun was shining and gave promise of a bright, spring day. (See published report page 84)

After a bowl of Force breakfast cereal, the time dragged a little until it was necessary to tidy up for church. Today's service was at noon. The church was filled to overflowing, to quote from the local newspaper report:

Everything, weather included, combined to make the day a great success. Two great incentives helped – the dinner and dance were in the beautiful, new Village Hall
And the presence of a large number of Mr. Marriot's employees who had built the hall.
Mr. and Mrs. Marriot accompanied them.

George   Ernie   Dick   Arnold   Frank   Jack
Timms   Herbert   Sollis   Wright   Harris   Harris

Ken   Alan   Walter   Harry   Harvey   Larry   Harry   Harry   Tom
Wells   Sollis   Preston   Cambray   Curtis   Luckett   Bedwell   Cole   Clements

George   John   Fred   Bill   Tom   Alf   Tom   Earnest   Bert   George   Albert   Archie   Mr   Fred
Hall   Herbert   Pitts   Hall   Preston   Herbert   Herbert   Curtis   Cole   Garratt   Witchell   Witchell   Thoms   Harris

Harvey   Jim   Baden   Bob   John   Canon   Rev.   Dr   George   Caleb   Rev.   George   Leslie   Jim
Sollis   Tuck   Arthurs   Tye   Thorn   Emeris   Sloane   Cheatle   Berry   Stratford   Warner   Faulkner   Hands   Sollis

Mr H. James   Walter
Barrett   Tufnell

The club members, headed by a new flag, and the Chedworth Silver Band, marched in procession. Again the large congregation can be congratulated in the hearty singing of favourite hymns – it was inspiring. The Reverend E.C. Hanson, rector of Shipton Oliffe, read the lesson and gave an address on "A perfect man."

Feeling quite proud and adult, Jim allowed his marching to relax and fell out of step a few times. So many of the marchers had been drilled in army routine and they swung along, heads held high, basking in the admiring looks of their womenfolk who had gathered in groups to watch the spectacle. The girls giggled a bit but it was easy to perceive they felt a little awkward about being excluded from this mans' world.

In time to the stirring marches played by the band, they processed down the village, did a smart right turn at the bottom, quick-stepped up the back lane and "fell out" at The Village Hall.

Before filing in to the building, Mr. Butt, the photographer from Bourton-on-the-Water arranged the club members into a closely-packed group. Then, after making much play of dashing backwards and forwards between them and his tripod mounted, plate camera, which he adjusted by poking his head under the black curtain which screened the lens, he stood beside it and pressed the plunger. This produced a sulphurous flash and committed the restless crowd to an image for posterity.

Inside the hall, the trestle tables were set out in rows, headed by a special one for the dignitaries. Seated at last, the real festivities of the day began in earnest. Foaming jugs of Garnes' best bitter served by Alf Francis and his colleagues from Burford, slopped their contents into the glasses of the eager diners. Youths and boys were encouraged to sup some "mans' drink". Jim was apprehensive and after deciding that he didn't like it, was regaled with Ginger Beer.

Great barons of salt beef were decimated; never did food taste so fine.

CORONATION DAY – MAY 12TH 1937

CORONATION 1937 – FANCY DRESS (Village Hall in background)

Back Row Jim Lazenby, Bob Browning, Doreen Lazenby, Pat Busson, Muriel Smith, Kathleen Parker, Mary Faulkner, Margaret Griffin, Peggy Sollis

Front Row Michael Arthurs, Joyce Sollis, R Tuck, Bridget Arkell, John Clements, Hester Clements, Ron Keylock, Jack Sollis G Tuck

CORONATION DAY – MAY 12TH 1937

Masters David and
Jonathan Wingfield,
'Nanny' Clark,
Betty Stocks and
Baden Arthurs

Coronation Day Parade through
Great Barrington

Prize Presentation
Mrs M. E. G. R. Wingfield,
Col Wingfield facing camera

FANCY DRESS – CORONATION DAY
Left to Right Gerard Lobb, Ben Sollis,
Cecil Deane, Cliff Bennett, Harold Sampson

To record this event correctly, I feel it only proper to reproduce the ensuing published report. But let me first observe that the toast list provides a perfect example of the village hierarchy. (See section at the end of the book)

It was a great pity that on this occasion, Colonel Wingfield was unable to attend because of a chill. Nevertheless, it was graced by the presence of Colonel Hurst, whose estate, the parish of Little Barrington and encompassing land on the south of the River Windrush adjoined the Great Barrington land, and extended to Burford, where he was Lord of the Manor.

The men, having now quaffed their fill of ale had somehow to concentrate on playing cricket.

Jim, with his usual companions, went up to the cricket pitch to watch their fathers, uncles and elder brothers perform. As usual, his grandfather was umpiring and somehow his father had been persuaded to play. Tom Lazenby could either amass a good score by hard hitting or was watched, returning quickly from the crease after failing to connect with the first ball, by a very unhappy and embarrassed son.

The cricket pitch was directly inside the stone-pillared, iron gates opening into the Deer Park up the Rissington road.

Uniquely, it was fenced in and protected by high wooden hurdles, which kept the deer off it. Several of these hurdles had to be removed, both to allow access and for the fielders to be able to retrieve those balls that went beyond them. When a batsman was in form outfielders were placed beyond the hurdles, lurking there and hoping to catch the next six when it came. The ultimate prowess was achieved by the fielder who, judging the ball, would land the other side of his fence, ran to the nearest gap, circled back and still caught his man out.

The loudest cheers were reserved for the batsman who could repeatedly punish the ball and rattle it into the big beech trees standing near the Park wall.

Members of the Arthurs' family feigned great style. When Baden, the clerk to Mr. Radway the estate agent, felt particularly pleased one day he headed the team down to The Fox Inn and consumed with magnanimity, ordered a quart of beer for them. Inevitably he acquired the nickname, "Quart Arthurs". His wife was Pat and when his son Michael was born the three were irreverently named "Quart, Pat and Pint". He was also one of the few people in the village with a car – a Singer Bantam. This enjoyed a reputation. He had parked it in a field and on returning with his girlfriend, found that the herd of cows there had taken a liking to it. The bodywork was canvas and they'd enjoyed stripping much of it away, so disclosing the ash frames to which it was attached; a terrible sequel to a romantic venture.

Though beaten, but only by allowing extra time, and so feeling that honour was satisfied, everyone ran, walked and skipped back down to the village.

Here they divided, surprisingly few going down to The Fox, most making their way to the fair and to finish off the beer still available.

The fair came alive. The showmen, the stallholders and even the mystical fortune-teller, who had felt themselves excluded from the village festivities, now acquired a third dimension. Ruddy-faced men, encouraged by their peers and dared by their families, queued to pay out their sixpences and crack a few coconuts.

The most powerful ones tried and tried again to "ring the bell". This contraption consisted of a pad which, when struck very hard, would cause a visible, metal projectile to travel up a calibrated scale. Onlookers could see exactly how far up it went. At the top of this twenty-foot erection was a bell. When it was struck, everyone cheered. Unlike most side-shows, there were no prizes. The elation of achieving it was reward enough. Unknown to his clients, the proprietor was able to adjust the effort required, so that it was quite possible for him to allow a puny contestant to "ring the bell" to the disbelief of the assembled crowd.

Again and again the long-handled wooden beetle would come crashing down whilst more and more money changed hands; side-bets were cashed.

Jim was with his grandfather, who was keeping his eye on the whole scene. Not the time to have a go at the cigarette booth!

BARRINGTON CRICKET TEAMS

BARRINGTON
LADIES CRICKET TEAM

Back Row Park Cook, Gertie Sollis, Connie Woodley,
Park Housemaid, Grace Stocker, Ethel Pitts,
Muriel Barnes, Mr Barrett
Front Row Gladys Saunders, Kathy Hall, Gwen Smith

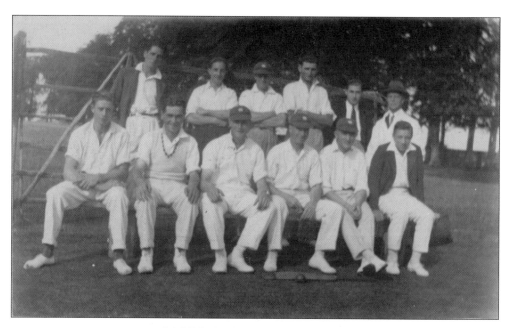

BARRINGTON CRICKET TEAM

Back Row Fred Clifford, Jim Hall, Ben Sollis, Jack Harris, Park Hall-boy, Mr Barrett
Front Row Norman Barnes, Harold Sampson, Dick Sollis, ?, Ben Sollis, ?

"Here, have some of this rock" was the inevitable offer and it was really good too, if you could forget the manner of its making and could find some handy stone to break it atop the stone wall.

Groups of men formed, mostly by the "beer tent". Men from far-flung farms and neighbouring villages. Friends, the majority, closely or distantly related, some that only met on this annual occasion.

"'Ello Caleb, 'ow bist?"

"I be alright, 'ow bist thee? Yeant sin thee since last time. 'Ow's the garden bin? 'Ad a couple of good litters of pigs this year".

The children were now being ignored and the church clock could be heard striking seven o'clock. Jim decided that it was past time he should be home and, tired and happy, he took his leave.

It had been a wonderful day. What a long time, a whole year before the next club day.

Mr Barrett in 'Retirement'

CHAPTER SEVEN

The next day it was back to school, a last look at the "fair" people who were already well advanced in the preparations for departure, and at the end of school lessons, wonderment that all was cleared and the village restored to its usual peace.

It would seem forever before the next and final red-letter day of the childrens' calendar arrived. This again, centred on the new Village Hall, but they must wait until December.

The completion and opening of this superb building marked the last of the activities and memorable festivities, which celebrated the bi-centenary of the Squire's family's ownership of the estate 1735–1935.

Monday, August 19th 1935 had been given over to feasting, drinking and organised merry-making, concluded by a firework display in front of the mansion, and what a display! Huge fire-work cameos had been erected, massive rockets, veritable mortar-bomb-like emplacements were readied and, after sundown, the whole community present, the skies erupted with unbelievable explosions, shrieks and colours, whilst four cameos were lit to reveal fiery, twenty foot high, head and shoulder likenesses of the first and present squires and their ladies. The whole, far outdoing the childrens' enjoyment of the previous flag-waving, sticky buns, days off school celebrations of the less important George V Silver Jubilee. The only pity being that no commemorative mugs were given to mark it. (See report in appendix page 82)

Some of the activities
celebrating
Jubilee Day
George V
1910–1935

Left – Col Chetwynd-Stapylton
Centre – Mr. A. E. Gibbs and
Archdeacon Cross
The 'Bowser' and barn at rear,
now demolished

Doreen   John   Grace   Philip   Jim   Tom   Hester
Lazenby Clements Bennet   Hands   Lazenby Jennings Clements
                 The Adams Twins   Robert
                   (Sherborne)   Clements

The building itself could grace a town community. Stage, with full curtains and floodlights, large, polished wood dance floor, gallery, cloakrooms, committee room, kitchens and toilets.

Regular dances to real band music, whist drives in the Committee Room, stage performances by quite remarkable local talent, school plays, piano recitals, string quartets, skirmishes with the fascinating pianola, which magically, played an extensive range of music simply by using foot pedals to rotate long rolls of perforated canvas. Even cinema showings by the Burford Cinema Management, assured the locals of ongoing entertainment. Bob Arnold, (Tom Forest of The Archers) made an early appearance there much to the disquiet of Jim's grandfather, who pronounced on his act as being, "Not quite the thing for Barrington" (too risqué).

Later during World War II, it was highly favoured by quite famous stage personalities and a big-band leader, Ronnie Pleydell, who were unfortunate enough to be serving in the RAF at Little Rissington, to the benefit of all concerned in the locality.

It had also superseded the school premises for yet another eagerly awaited day "The Christmas Tree" or I suppose, more properly, "The Christmas Treat".

Mrs. Wingfield, the Squire's lady, undertook the unenviable task of advancing on Hamleys with a comprehensive list of every boy and girl living on the estate, and buying most appropriate presents for everyone.

The occasion, just before Christmas, followed a time-honoured pattern. The children, sent home early from school to change into their best clothes, came, accompanied by their mothers, to the hall and seated themselves all around the perimeter, leaving a vast empty dance floor, at the head of which, in front of the stage, were set up two big trestle tables. A large, fully dressed Christmas tree dominated the whole. After a settling period and a suitable welcome by the lady herself, she, assisted by hovering servants, proceeded to distribute the individually wrapped presents.

Each one named and quite obviously, carefully selected, some fifty or sixty separate packages. Excitement mounted.

"Margaret Cambray", "John Clements", "Irene Cole", "Jim Lazenby", and so the names continued. As each child was called, he or she hurried the formidable length or breadth of the highly polished dance floor, head down to avoid slipping and stumbling as had some of the others, and stopped with scarce disguised trepidation in front of the creaking tables. After some appropriate words of wisdom and greeting, they were then handed their presents.

By now, suffused with embarrassment and confusion, the girls had then to make a bob and the boys to salute, before rushing back to their parents, exploring the present and comparing it with those of brothers, sisters and friends. The salute came quite naturally to the boys, as it was requisite that they should always salute when meeting either the squire or his lady anywhere at all and at all times. Failure to do so would be reported to school for action by the headmaster.

This long and protracted giving and receiving ended, the childrens' attention was then fixed on a huge tin of sweets now being opened. Knowing what was to come, they then entrusted their presents to their parents and prepared for the forthcoming mêlée.

"Come along, children", was the cry and the lady reached her hands into the tin and pulled out great handfuls of sweets, which she then proceeded to throw all over the dance floor. The higher she threw and the farther she threw, the more they rattled and spread.

Not wrapped sweets, but large, glittering, sugar-speckled, assorted flavour pear drops, which gained something by picking up an extra coating of French chalk with which the floor was regularly treated.

What a scramble! Children rushing wildly around gathering them quickly in sweaty, sticky, little hands. The competition was keen, but even the youngest were allowed their share. Soon after, the Vicar and the schoolmaster tendered suitable thanks and appreciation, and encouraged a hearty rendering of "For she's a jolly good fellow".

The party was over.

Barrington Village Hall

Wingfield Crest
over doorway of
Village Hall
Commemorative
Date 1735–1935

'Thatched Cottage' now tiled, was home for Jim Smith the retired village blacksmith

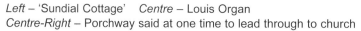

Left – 'Sundial Cottage'   *Centre* – Louis Organ
Centre-Right – Porchway said at one time to lead through to church

AN INTERESTING HISTORY OF GREAT BARRINGTON SCHOOL
COMPILED BY MR A. E. GIBBS CLOSE TO HIS RETIREMENT IN 1959

Up till, and even some time after, the combining of the Boys and Girls Schools some children at least came to Great Barrington from Taynton, Windrush and Great Rissington for their "schooling", which could not have amounted to much as they were often absent for a great variety of reasons, sometimes for long periods, and many were frequently "sacked", temporarily at least, by the Master or Mistress for prolonged truancy! The flies in the ointment of this happy state of affairs were (a) the loss of some mysterious documents known as "Tickets", which had a cash value, and (b) the even more serious loss of precious attendance marks which would delay the receipt of the much desired Certificate of honourable discharge!

Little Barrington probably kept pace, more or less, with Great Barrington with its own schooling facilities for the records show that "by 1874 the Little Barrington School had been altered and a certificated teacher appointed."

Taynton, Windrush and Great Rissington obviously also acquired schools for all their children at sometime; the Windrush one existing until 1915, when the number of children there had dropped to 15, and they were transferred to Great Barrington.

The present school building has changed little since 1899 and, on the whole, it has served its purpose very well, but it now seems likely that it is about to receive a "face lift" and enter upon a new era, taking its place with other comparable small Primary Schools of this day and age.

But it is perhaps the human side of the past that is most absorbing. Apart from the Mistresses, there have been only three Masters since 1845, a period of 113 years. This may not be unique, but it is certainly remarkable. The first Master, Alfred Baylis, served from 1845 till 1882, a period of 37 years. He was followed in 1883 by Henry James Barrett, who served till 1925, a period of 42 years.

(Present day children will envy those of 1882 in at least one thing, as there was a long "vacation" of over four months from August 1882, when Mr. Baylis retired, till January 1883 when Mr. Barrett was appointed – either the Managers of those days being hard to please or suitable Masters scarce!)

I came in December 1925 and hope to complete just short of 34 years.

My interview with the School Managers is still very fresh in my mind. Twenty six teachers had applied for the post. The Education Office at Gloucester whittled this number down to three, of whom only two finally faced the Managers (the other having obtained a Headship elsewhere just before the interview). As it was 42 years since the last Head Teacher had been appointed the Managers must have found the business of choosing a new one a somewhat unfamiliar duty, and I suspect that they were probably almost as uncomfortable as the candidates themselves! As I remember it, the issue seemed to hang on two main questions:
(a) could I make a hundred at cricket, and
(b) how did I think the cost of living in Barrington would compare with the cost of living in Birmingham (where I had been teaching).

My answer to the first unfortunately had to be in the negative, and, as I was not yet married, I had only very vague notions about the second, so I have often thought that I got the job because my answers must have been slightly less unsatisfactory than those of my rival! However that may be, I have no real regrets that things turned out as they did for it was the beginning of 34 years of satisfying, and, I hope, useful work.

And now to return to the Schools Log Books.

The one kept for the old Girls School reveals the names of two Mistresses. The first was Mrs. Anne Maria Clarke, who was already here when records started in 1873, and who left in December 1880. She was followed by Miss Moss in January 1881. The change seems to have been quite uneventful, as there is nothing to mark it, except a change of handwriting in the Log Book, and the beginning of some rather quaint examples of spelling, e.g. "holydays" for "holidays" which really does take us back a bit!

The Log Book entries of the first Master give an impression of a conscientious, hard working, man, who ruled his school firmly, but, who, towards the end, began to lose the battle with his boys who were "booked" more and more often for truancy, inattention, bad work, impertinence, and, dare we whisper it, bad language.

With the coming of the second Master entries become much less intimate and tend more and more to be a record of routine matters, but it is interesting to note that, for many more years, the Summer Holidays were referred to as Harvest Holidays, and their commencement and duration were entirely dependent upon the weather and the state of the crops. How the boys must have hoped for fine weather round about the end of July and welcomed rain towards the end of August as bad weather invariably prolonged the holiday for another week or so!

But though the Log Books make it possible to form only a shadowy impression of the Masters and Mistresses of the 1800's the picture of the children and their school days is perfectly clear. On the whole the girls were perhaps not so lucky as the boys, because, whereas the boys were often excused school for such exciting things as "beating the pheasants" and for employment at fishing parties, the girls could only hope for permitted release when their mothers were "confined". But, as that was fairly often, may be, after all, the girls were fairly content!

For the rest let the following selection of quotes from the early days of the Log Books speak for themselves:

1874   July 20th   Ann _____ returned to school after a months absence. Mother confined.

1875   April 19th   Jos _____ stayed away all day after leave had been refused and against wish of his parents having been hired by Edward _____ to look after his horse while grazing on the roadside. This boy is between 8 and 9 years of age.

June 5th   From H.M.I.'s Report – "The singing of the girls should improve or the payment under article 19(A)2 may be withheld."

June 22nd   Mary _____ leave to nurse baby, Mother out hay-making.

August 2nd   Removed Henry _____'s name from the roll as he neither came to school nor sent any message other than "He should not come."

1876   May 11th   Sarah Ann _____ absent to fetch Dr. _____ brother bitten by a horse.

1877   January 19th   G _____ punished severely for untruthfulness concerning his home lessons.

February 16th   Harriet _____ very idle in learning particularly Arithmetic.

July 19th   W _____ absent again this morning. He starts with the other scholars from Taynton but leaves them on the way.

August 3rd   Harvest very late this year. Have usually broken up by this time.

August 13th   Harvest operations commencing – many of the boys away.

November 21st   Received note that B _____ had, the last few days, been playing Truant, and that his parents did not know of it. Boy caned.

December 21st   Wm. _____ absent all this week, reported sick but doubtful.

1878   January 16th   Gave some Second Standard Boys some Home lessons for the first time - _____ In a few minutes Chas. _____ returned with his saying Mother told him to take "that thing" back. She would not have it there at his home.

June 24th   Some mischievous boys are continually turning off the nuts of the Desks and seats and much trouble is caused in trying to find out the offenders.

1879   January 13th   Had occasion to punish Louis _____ with two stripes of the cane for disobedience, was waylaid by his mother _____ She caused a great disturbance in the street and dispensed vituperation freely.

March 10th   William _____ was most perversely disobedient and defiant: after a good flogging and threatened expulsion from the Choir he came round to better behaviour.

April 30th   William _____ and Frederick _____ were punished with the cane being found out in, and shown up by, the Teacher for obtaining the answers to their sums <u>dishonestly</u>.

1880   May 7th   Re-arranged desks so as to leave space for a class on the floor.

June 2nd   Emma _____ remarkably dull and stupid all the week.

November 4th   Closed School all day to enable the girls to attend Church which was re-opened after restoration (Note The boys had only half a day for this!)

1881   January 20th   Snow storm ceased last evening. Roads in neighbourhood blocked in places by snow drifts from 4 to 8 ft. deep: a few boys came.

April 27th   Park Day. The children of all the schools had a holiday for Wood Picking.

June 17th   The whole of 1st Class lost their Tickets for the week for rude and noisy behaviour on leaving school Monday morning.

July 22nd   Ada _____'s name taken off register she having been dismissed for bad behaviour and her parents insulting behaviour and refused to punish the child.

December 9th   Flannel gown finished.

1882   March 3rd   The Attendance Officer called today for the first time, he said his reason for not coming before was owing to his ignorance of the existence of the school.

1883   January 9th   Had occasion to reprove one of the younger children for telling an untruth – this led to a school discourse to all the Scholars on the sin of lying.

December 14th   8 and 10 First Class boys had holiday (4 days) for the purpose of beating.

1886   July 2nd   Hay-making Notice issued by the Attendance Committee to allow boys over 8 to help in the Hay field. The notice to be in force for 3 weeks.

1887   January 21st   Floods over causeway to Little Barrington. No boys could come from that village.

1888   February 14th   Deep snow – did not open school for a whole week.

And finally, an up-to-date entry that shows, as well as anything could, clear progress in at least one direction:

1958   November 12th   Health Visitor carried out hair inspection – all clear.
(This is the last time this "ritual" will take place as the need for it is now well and truly a thing of the past).   Arthur E. Gibbs

APPENDIX

1936–1937 SUNDAY SCHOOL OUTINGS

GREAT BARRINGTON.

SUNDAY SCHOOL CHILDREN'S OUTING. —On Saturday, July 25th, the annual outing arranged for the Sunday School scholars was carried out. They started in motor coaches at 1.30 p.m., when rain was pouring down, and it seemed as if the weather might interfere with the enjoyment of the party, but, luckily, hardly any rain fell afterwards. They inspected the zoo at Kidlington, then finished with a nice tea. Then they journeyed to Oxford, where a rush was made on "Woolworth's," where the shillings supplied soon vanished. A visit to the Majestic Cinema was the next event, and the boys especially were pleased with a "wild west" picture, "Nevada." Another picture was "She shall have music," featuring Jack Hilton and his band. Altogether a very enjoyable day ended when they reached home at 8.30 p.m. Mothers and friends also took the opportunity to join in the outing, and they were very profuse in their thanks to Mrs. Lazenby for her excellent arrangements.

SCHOOL OUTING.—For some time the older scholars of Great Barrington C.E. School had been saving their pennies to pay for an outing to London, and this took place as stated in our last issue, on Wednesday, July 15th. Besides the children there were parents and friends who joined them, making a total of 61, of which 35 were children. At the start, when the motor coaches arrived, the weather looked very threatening and "macs" overcoats and umbrellas were taken. The coaches took them to Shipton (G.W.R.) Station, which they left at 9.40 a.m., for Paddington, and eager eyes looked out for anything of note, especially Huntley and Palmer's factory, Sutton's and Barr's flower beds, a distant view of Windsor Castle, and the numerous factories alongside the line for miles before reaching London. A large two-decker bus was waiting and they were driven to the Houses of Parliament, where they were met and welcomed by Mr. W. S. Morrison, K.C., M.P., the member for their own division. Then followed to many the most interesting part of the day, for Mr. Morrison showed them everything that appealed to old and young : the Terrace and the Thames rolling by, with ships and barges going out with the tide, and, to the delight of the youngsters, lowering their funnels as they reached the bridges. He then called attention to the action of the weather on the stones of the House, requiring continual renewing of the fabric. In the House of Commons he pointed out the Speaker's Chair, the Government benches, the distinguished visitors' gallery, where often the King when Prince of Wales, listened to the debates with arms resting on the clock. At the other end was the visitors' gallery, where the suffragettes chained themselves to the window bars in their appeal for Votes for Women. He traced the passing of a Bill and the voting on the third reading and pointed out where the "Ayes" and "Noes" passed to record their votes, with the four tellers watching and counting. In the House of Lords attention was called to the "Woolsack," on which the Lord Chancellor sits, and to the throne used by the King at the opening of Parliament. A visit to the noble Westminster Hall followed and some of the worm-eaten timbers were examined. They had been taken down and new st ig oak suitably treated put in their p   . It was an instructive and enjoy- a visit and at the end Mr. A. E. Gibbs, h dmaster, thanked Mr. Morrison heartily for the delightful talk. Mr. Morrison wished them a happy time and a safe return home. After leaving the House they were driven to the Zoo, a place of course beloved by the children especially. It may be mentioned that Colonel Wingfield, of Barrington Park, had sent free tickets for admission for all, and tickets also for the young ones to visit the Aquarium, an act very much appreciated. At 4.30 a splendid tea was enjoyed and, after allowing a time for digestion, the party were driven through the principal streets of the City, past the Horse Guards, with glimpses of Downing-street, St. Paul's, and Westminster Abbey, the Thames Embankment and Cleopatra's Needle and the Tower, and so back to Paddington to entrain for the return journey. A fast run to Oxford and then a rather slow, tedious journey to Shipton, enabled them to board the coaches for Barrington, which was reached about 10.30 p.m. A glorious day—the overcoats were left all day in the coach—and everything admirably arranged by Mr. Gibbs, to whom many thanks were given by all who had enjoyed an admirable outing.

SOCIAL FOR SUNDAY SCHOOL OUTING.

A fine spirit of co-operation made the social held in the Village Hall, Great Barrington, last Friday, a great success. Everyone seemed determined to do their best to help the funds, which were for a Sunday School outing. Refreshments came in from all sides, and the mothers of the Sunday School scholars acted as waitresses.

While the company assembled Mr. R. R. Arthurs officiated at the pianola, then at 7.30 came " Nursery Rhymes " from the younger children. Each one was dressed to the part and performed the appropriate action. Later on these children each gave a recitation. These were greatly enjoyed.

Three plays were given by the older children—" Our At 'Ome Day," in which Mrs. Snobson (Margaret Cambray), a newly rich lady, has an " At 'ome day " to satisfy her " educated " daughter (Irene Cole), to the the discomfiture of the servant Sabina (Betty Tufnell), only to find, after much preparation, that no one comes to the " At 'ome day." Another play by three girls was the very amusing gossip sketch, " Neighbours in Gooseberry Court," with Doreen Lazenby as *Amelia Copper*, Hester Clements as *Mrs. Dobbs*, and Peggy Sollis as *Mrs. Perkins*. Four boys acted " Dr. Diaculum " with great gusto and kept the audience in roars. J. Lazenby, *Dr. Diaculum* ; P. Hands, *Joshua* ; J. Clements, *Mr. Simpson* ; and Tom Jennings, the *Policeman*.

The three dances given by Mary Curtis were a great attraction. First there was a tap dance, then a Hungarian dance, and then the song and dance, " When I was Colour Blind "—all in costume.

Very hearty community singing was led by Mr. Roberts, a member of the Church Choir. Those officiating at the piano during the evening were Mr. Barrett, Mrs. Curtis, and Mrs. W. Hall.

Thanks to Mr. W. Baker's untiring efforts, the competition for a tea-set, given by Mr. J. Ball (Messrs. Hambidge, Burford), brought in £1 8s. This was won by Mrs. George Berry.

The other competition for a cake and shortbread, collected by Miss Hale and Betty Tufnell, brought in 8s. 11d. Mrs. J. Tidmarsh won the cake and Mrs. R. Preston the shortbread (also given by Mr. Ball).

Penny " fortunes " were on sale from a very realistic gipsy woman (Mrs. T. Herbert), and realised 7s. 8d. Donations amounted to 11s., and the sale of programmes (mainly hand-painted) to 5s. 9d. The Committee were most grateful to the Misses Deane-Drummond for their help with the programmes.

At the conclusion of the entertainment items the Rev. W. T. WARDLE proposed a hearty vote of thanks to Mrs. Lazenby for organising, and to all those who had taken part in the programme. He also thanked all who had come there to help the funds. Mrs. WINGFIELD seconded his proposal, remarking what patience must have been required to teach the children and how very enjoyable everything had been.

Mrs. LAZENBY replied thanking them for their appreciation and saying that her ambition this year was to take the children to the seaside again, but this time to a sandy beach. She thanked all who had helped to make the evening a success, among them Mr. Harvey Sollis, at the door, and Mr. T. Herbert ticket-collector. They were all very sorry Mr. George Berry was not well enough to be with them in his usual capacity as doorman, but everyone was glad he was getting better.

Amid loud applause Myrtle Cambray presented Mrs. Lazenby with a lovely bouquet of daffodils and tulips contributed to entirely by the Sunday School scholars. Mrs. Lazenby said Mr. Barrett deserved the flowers more than she did for teaching at Sunday School !

After refreshments, dancing began to the strains of The Sunnyside Accordian Band, and kept on till 1 a.m.

The result of the evening was most gratifying, receipts being £11 16s. 9d. expenses £3 12s. 11d., and the splendid amount is £8 3s. 10d. available for the outing fund.

GREAT BARRINGTON.

SUNDAY SCHOOL OUTING.—A most enjoyable time was spent on Friday, August 27th, by the Sunday school schoars, mothers and friends on their outing to Swindon. The two coaches started from the memorial, Great Barrington, at 12.45 and went by way of Lechlade and Highworth to Swindon, reaching Messrs Wills's tobacco factory at 2 p.m. Here most of the children and some of the mothers—a party of 22 in all —were put down for a tour over the Factory. The rest went on into Swindon and alighted at the station for shopping in the town, except for seven of the oldest boys—in charge of Mrs Lagerbry—who went on to the G.W.R. works for a tour of inspection. This lasted for two hours. One boy who had had his leg hurt a day or two before made the tour in a push chair, the first push chair which had ever been taken round the works. The boys could not fail to be interested in the marvellous machinery and tremendous engine " parts." but the noise was terrific and speech to one another impossible! The tobacco factory tour took an hour and a half and was most interesting, even for the youngest children. Then, at the end, each adult was presented with a souvenir tin of cigarettes and each child with a large bundle of cards. Then everyone met and enjoyed a good tea. After tea there was another hour and a half for shopping, and then the drive home by way of the White Horse Hills. The evening was perfect and the view from the top of the hill magnificent. After that the party returned home by way of Faringdon. Grateful thanks are due to the Rev. G. R. Parkinson and to all who helped so well towards this fund during the winter. Their reward must have been in hearing such glowing accounts of such a really happy day.

GREAT BARRINGTON.

PRESENTATION TO MR. H. J. BARRETT.

On Friday Mr. H. J. Barrett, the retiring headmaster of Great Barrington Church of England School, was presented with a gold watch and chain and an illuminated address by his old pupils and other friends, a large number of whom were present. There were over a hundred subscribers to the testimonial.

The Rev. G. R. Parkinson, Vicar, spoke of the many and varied ways in which Mr. Barrett had helped in the village, and on behalf of everybody who knew Mr. Barrett expressed regret on his retirement.

Colonel Wingfield, who made the presentation, also spoke of the good work which Mr. Barrett had done during his 43 years' service, and read letters from friends who had left the district regretting their absence and expressing appreciation of Mr. Barrett's record. He added that they were pleased that he was going to remain amongst them.

Mr. Barrett, in expressing his gratitude, gave instances of the kindness he had received from Colonel Wingfield and his father, and from many other persons during his long stay in the village.

The watch bore the following inscription: " Presented to Henry James Barrett, Headmaster of Great Barrington School, 1883-1925, in appreciation of long and valuable services," and the illuminated address contained the following: " A list of subscribers who contributed to the gold watch and chain presented to Mr. Henry James Barrett on his retirement from the headmastership of Great Barrington School on November 30, 1925, after 43 years' service. His old pupils and friends will always remember affectionately his faithful and devoted work amongst them in so many different capacities."

On Monday Mr. H. J. Barrett finished his work as headmaster of Great Barrington School, and at the conclusion of lessons in the afternoon the scholars assembled in the chief room and Miss Woods, assistant teacher, said they had met together to thank Mr. Barrett for the earnest and sympathetic work he had done in the past, to wish him a long and happy retirement, and to give him a small present.

Molly O'Reilly, one of the headmaster's pupils, made the presentation with a pretty little speech, thanking Mr. Barrett not only for his teaching, but for his kindness in every way. She handed him a silver inkstand, engraved, together with an artistically-executed list of the teachers and children who had subscribed.

Mr. Barrett, in thanking them very heartily, said he knew they had given in the right spirit— a wish to give him pleasure. This they had certainly done, and he should always value this token of their esteem. He would miss them more than he could express, and if ever they wanted help in any way he hoped they would come to him.

1935 JUBILEE CELEBRATIONS

GREAT BARRINGTON.

The Committee for carrying out the programme for the day must be very gratified at the marvellous way in which every event came off without a hitch of any kind, and to the great enjoyment of all. " Never had been such a happy day " was the general verdict. and the glorious weather helped to make it so.

At 12.30 a Thanksgiving Service was held in the Church. when a large congregation sang " with heart and voice," God save the King. and listened to an appropriate address on the life and work of His Majesty, given by the Vicar. Colonel Wingfield read the Lessons.

Dinner was served to 85 men in the School at 1.30 p.m.. Colonel Wingfield in the chair. Everything was well done and everyone thoroughly enjoyed their beef. beer and baccy.

The Chairman proposed the health of The King. which received musical honours. He traced the 25 years of anxiety and stress through which His Majesty had gone through triumphantly and had endeared himself more than ever to his people.

The Rev. G. R. Parkinson proposed the health of Colonel Wingfield, who, he said, might be compared in some ways to His Majesty. for, like the King, he was a sympathetic ruler of his village subjects, and like him also had a bevy of stalwart sons to carry on the traditions of the family. Loud applause and musical honours followed.

The the Chairman gave them the toast of The Committee who had worked so long and so hard for the success of the day. Especially must they thank Mr. Gibbs, their chairman, and Mr. B. R. Arthurs, their hon. secretary and treasurer.

Mr. Gibbs replied by saying that with such a committee they possessed. he had found the work both interesting and pleasant. He must mention the splendid way that Mr. Barnes had acted throughout. Mr. Arthurs also said that it had been a pleasure to serve them and to arrange the items for, he hoped, a memorable day. The lady helpers and cook were also thanked.

SPORTS RESULTS

BARRINGTON'S FAST GRANDFATHERS

Men Excel at Hat Trimming

Mr. T. Clements, Senr., won the grandfather's race at Great Barrington on Monday.

Sports winners were: —

100 yards flat, boys 11 years and over: C. Tidmarsh; 80 yards, boys under 11: P. Hands; 100 yards, girls 11 and over: M. Long; 80 yards, girls under 11: P. Sollis; infant boys: E. Ball; infant girls: D. Lazenby.

Obstacle race, 11—15: D. Cole.

Skipping race, all girls: H. Clements; egg and spoon race, boys: J. Lazenby; girls: M. Long.

Sack race: J. Clements; wheelbarrow race: Hands and Dodd; tie-legged race, girls: Long and Hands; tie-legged race, boys: J. Lazenby and J. Clements.

Adults events: —100 yards flat race (handicap): B. Sollis; grandfathers' race: T. C. Clements, senr.; 880 yards handicap: B. Reynolds; egg and spoon race, lades: Miss Griffin; hat trimming, ladies: Mrs. Whitlock.

Obstacle race: W. Preston; musical chairs on cycles: Miss Griffin; 120 yards hurdles: B. Reynolds.

Hat trimming, men: B. Reynolds; throwing cricket ball: F. Clifford; 100 yards: girls over 16: Miss M. Griffin.

GREAT BARRINGTON NOTABLE FOR ITS DECORATIONS

As a whole the Cotswold villages did not bear comparison with those in the Vale of White Horse in the matter of decorations, with one notable exception, Great Barrington. Here streamers hung across the street; almost every house had its trimmings.

In a cricket match between men and their fair challengers scoring did not seem to be the main point; runs were often sacrificed for the sake of a hearty laugh.

Grandfathers and grandmothers had special races in the sports programme.

Earlier there had been a Church service, followed by a luncheon in the School for the men, who had no complaints to offer about the hospitality extended.

The women and children had tea; more sports followed, and towards dusk there was an exodus to Windrush to see the bonfire.

1937 CORONATION DAY

GREAT BARRINGTON.

At 11 o'clock a broadcast of the cere-
mony was made in the Church until
12.30, when a short service was held until
the broadcast of the crowning of the
Queen was heard.

Dinner to 70 male adults was served
in the new Village Hall, very kindly
lent by Colonel Wingfield and this was
greatly appreciated and enjoyed. The
hall was gaily decorated. As Colonel
Wingfield and family were in London,
the Vicar, the Rev. G. R. Parkinson was
chairman. The loyal and other toasts
were honoured.

At 2.15 all the children were presented
with Union Jacks by Masters David and
Johnathon Wingfield, in the absence of
their parents. All the children, waving
their flags, and folowed by the whole of
the fancy dress competitors, marched
through the village and back to the field,
where the dresses were judged by popular
vote.

In the children's class a tiny child
as "Sunflower," was easily first. Other
notable costumes were "Darby and

Joan " and the " Policeman." Prizes
were won by G. Tuck, B. Arkell, H.
Clements, J. Lazenby, R. Browning, J.
Clements, Misses Griffin, and Miss N.
Faulkner.

There were only two adult entries and
they were both very nice. Result : 1
Miss M. Griffin, Queen Elizabeth, 2
Miss M. Faulkner, Dolly Varden.

After this an adjournment was made
to the Hall where each received a souvenir
mug and box of chocolates from the
hands of Masters Wingfield.

Then followed tea to women and children, about 120, waited on by gentlemen
waiters.

Sports were then carried out, first for
the children, followed by the adults'
events. Results were :

100 yards flat.— 1 B. Sollis, 2 W. Preston, 3 W. Tufnell.

Egg and spoon, ladies.—1 Miss M.
Griffin, 2 Miss Hale, 3 Miss Jennings.

880 yards flat.—1 W. Preston, 2
Wilfred Preston, 3 D. Cole.

Hat trimming, ladies.—1 Mrs. Browning, 2 Miss M. Griffin, 3 Miss Hale.

100 yards, girls under 16.—1 Miss
Griffin, 2 Miss Wall, 3 Miss Long.

120 yards, hurdle race.—1 B. Sollis,
2 W. Preston, 3 A. Warner.

Hat trimming, men.—1 J. Tuck, 2
A. V. Sollis, 3 A. Richards.

Obstacle race.—1 W. Preston, 2 B.
Sollis.

Blindfold driving, men.—1 Miss Griffin and A. V. Sollis, 2 Miss Long and F.
Ballard.

Ditto, ladies.—1 J. Cole and T. Hayward, 2 Miss Sanders and Mr. Barnes, 3
Miss Smith and J. Parrott.

Musical chairs on bicycles.—1 J. Parrott, 2 D. Cole, 3 C. Ballard.

Throwing cricket ball.—1 F. Clifford,
2 B. Sollis, 3 A. V. Sollis.

After the King's speech, the rain
began to fall gently, so everybody
went into the capacious hall, where
the prizes were presented by Mr. H. J.
Barrett. Owing to the rain, the fire-
work display was postponed. Refreshments were served to all until 10 o'clock.
Community singing was indulged in and
a very jolly time was spent. Then followed a dance until 1 a.m. and the polished
floor gave great pleasure to the dancers.
Music was supplied by the radio-gram
of Mr. B. R. Arthurs. So ended what
inhabitants state, as the best day they
had ever enjoyed. It might be added
that the whole village was tastefully
decorated, every house having its bunt-
ing, flags, shields, etc.

Bicentenary Celebrations at Great Barrington.

Colonel Wingfield Entertains the Village.

A Memorable Day.

August 19th is a date that will be long remembered by the inhabitants of Great Barrington, for on Monday, August 19th, of this year, Colonel Wingfield, of Barrington Park, entertained all the villagers and any others who had been connected with the estate. This was to mark the 200th anniversary of his ancestors' accession to the estate. Cards of invitation were sent out to all eligible, the result being that a most enjoyable time was spent by all.

Women and children were invited at 2.30 to an entertainment provided by Tom Hay and consisting of a Punch and Judy show, a ventrilcquist, a conjurer, and comic singers. Then 298 sat down to a bountiful tea. Meanwhile gramophones, with loud speakers, enlivened the proceedings with appropriate music.

After tea, the VICAR, the Rev. G. R. Parkinson, thanked Colonel and Mrs. Wingfield for their great kindness and said that very few knew of the many acts Colonel Wingfield did for Church and village. This was very heartily cheered.

At 5.30 the men assembled to hear another entertainment before their supper, which was served in a huge marquee. A company of 204 sat down and thoroughly enjoyed the good things provided.

At the end, Colonel WINGFIELD, in proposing the toast of his Majesty the King in his Silver Jubilee year, said he was quite sure the King did not celebrate his Jubilee in a spirit of self-glorification, but for the good of trade and for people to forget their troubles, and to get people to come from abroad and spend their money over here. He thought it a great pity that the verse of the National Anthem which commenced " Thy choicest gifts in store On him be pleased to pour " was not always sung.

Then Mr. H. HOULTON, of Taynton, as the tenant farmer longest connected with the estate, proposed the health of Colonel and Mrs. Wingfield. He said he had been asked to do this as his family had farmed for more than 50 years. No doubt, he said, many could speak more eloquently, but he must say they had a very fine landlord, one who studied them in every way and always gave a helping hand in any time of adversity. Might he enjoy good health and reign for many years.

This was received with loud cheers and the singing of the old refrain, " For they are jolly good people."

In returning thanks, Colonel WINGFIELD said that Mr. Houlton mentioned that he had lived a quarter of 200 years, but he was sorry to find that he himself had lived nearly a third of that time. It was at the end of March, 1926, that he discovered that the estate was purchased by his ancestor, Lord Chancellor Talbot, on August 19th, 1735, so he had been looking forward to that day's entertainment for those nine years. He thought it would be a

great opportunity to have a celebration of the bicentenary. Long ago he had been told that the greatest happiness in life came from making and seeing others happy. It was seldom that they got q chance of glorification in the country. It was not in any spirit of vain-glory that that party was held, but just as a chance to welcome those connected with the estate (in the part as well as the present) to (should he call it ?) a happy family party. He hoped they would really enjoy the day, especially the youngsters outside the tent, and be able to remember it and talk of it all their lives.

Mr. E. W. RADWAY, agent, said he could not let the occasion go by without asking them to drink the Colonel's health on behalf of his employees. In every way they were treated sympathetically and kindly by their employer and he wished to express on their behalf their thanks to him. Needless to say, many strange events had happened during the 200 past years, and no one could possibly imagine what would take place in the future, but he hoped that at the end of another bicentenary descendants of the Colonel's family might still be in possession of that lovely estate.

After thanking them, Colonel WINGFIELD asked them to go out and watch a display of fireworks just in front of the house.

There Brock's men had been busy erecting set pieces of fireworks, causing much excitement, especially amongst the younger members. Besides innumerable rockets, there were Roman candles galore, cocks fighting, boxes boxing, an acrobat tumbling, the Falls of Niagara, and then the portrait of Lord Chancellor Talbot, 1735, and those of Colonel and Mrs. Wingfield, 1935. Needless to say the latter was received with loud cheers and clapping.

To conclude a " live " picture of the King was exhibited. This was accompanied most impressively by the singing of " God save the King " by the hundreds of spectators present.

Three cheers were then given, on the call of Mr. BARRETT, for Colonel and Mrs. Wingfield and family, in reply to which the COLONEL hoped that all had enjoyed the festivities and wished them " Good Night."

Colonel and Mrs. Wingfield at both the tea and supper were accompanied by their children, Miss Mary, Master Mervyn, Master Charles and Miss Elizabeth. Other members of the family present were Major and Mrs. W. Wingfield, Sir Charles Wingfield, Mr. Tim Wingfield, Captain G. Wingfield and Miss Ella Wingfield.

BARRINGTON RECORDS
Thousand Tons Per Acre Shortage

MR. BARRETT'S OBSERVATIONS

A thousand tons of rain per acre shortage since 1932.

That is the startling record of Great Barrington, as disclosed by Mr. H. J. Barrett, the Meteorological Expert, who for no less than forty years has furnished the Ministry every month with a report of each day's rainfall as recorded by his gauge.

The present abnormal weather makes his records particularly interesting to peruse.

They show that the wettest year in that district since 1888 was 1912, when there was a fall of 41.57 inches. The driest year was 1921, when only 17.25 inches fell. Other comparatively dry years were 1893 with 19.73 inches, 1902 20.06 inches, 1898 20.91 inches. Last year had 22.16 inches, whilst the average rainfall is in the neighbourhood of 30 inches.

During the whole time only one month had no rain at all, and that was February of 1891. October of the following year made up for that with the tropical fall of 6¼ inches.

It is unlikely that anyone shares with Mr. Barrett the distinction of having voluntarily kept and recorded a rain gauge for such a long period as forty years. It is natural that the Authorities should appreciate his excellent service. Some time ago, in recognition, he was invited to be a Fellow of the Meteorologic Society, but being content with the satisfaction which his achievement has given him he refused the invitation.

Mr. Barrett's long meteorological service not his only record. For the surprising period of 43 years he was Master of the Great Barrington School, from which he retired in 1925.

Born and partly educated at Abingdon he later went to the Diocesan College at Culham for Teacher's Training. On completion of his course there, he came to Great Barrington School, where despite many offers of more lucrative posts, he remained throughout his teaching career.

Now in his retirement he has the happiness of looking back. He knows the history of almost every one in the village. Fathers and mothers, grown up and growing families were his pupils. He is known and affectionately regarded by them all.

And though he is 74 he is still a young man and likely to exceed by many years half a century of meteorological records.

GREAT BARRINGTON
Jumble Sold to Swell Bell Fund

A jumble sale for the Church Bell Fund held last Saturday realised £13 12s. 6d., and there is every possibility that this total should be increased, for the goods were displayed for sale during the week at the Post Office. The helpers at the sale were: Mrs. Wingfield, Mrs. Keylock, Mrs. Lazenby, Nurse Worcester, Mrs. Arthurs, the Misses Griffin, Miss Woodley, Mrs. Bartlett (Senr.), Mrs. W. Bartlett, Mrs. Browning. Mrs. Berry was in charge of the teas.

MINISTER TO THE HOLY SEE
Sir Charles Rhys Wingfield's Appointment

Sir Charles John Fitzroy Rhys Wingfield, third son of the late Mr. Edward Rhys Wingfield, of Barrington Park, has been appointed Envoy Extraordinary and Minister Plenipotentiary to the Holy See.

Sir Charles, who is a brother of Lieut.-Colonel Mervyn E. G. Rhys Wingfield, of Barrington Park, has been Envoy Extraordinary and Minister Plenipotentiary at Oslo since 1929. He was born in 1877, educated at Charterhouse, and after serving as a Captain in the Royal Fusiliers, entered the Diplomatic Service in 1901.

He has since served in Paris, Athens, Berlin, Madrid, Oslo and Lisbon, before becoming First Secretary in Vienna, where he was stationed when war broke out. In 1923 he was transferred to Brussels, and three years later to Rome, where he twice acted as Chargé d'Affaires. In 1928 he was appointed British Minister at Bangkok, and a year later was transferred to Oslo. He received a knighthood last year.

BARRINGTON CLUB DAY.

Benefit Society's Jubilee.

Same Secretary for 50 Years.

Though the old-established Club Days are rapidly dying out, Barrington decided to keep up the old custom, though very near to the Coronation festivities. Many thought it would be better to drop it this time, but as it was the Jubilee of the Club, being founded in 1887, the Committee decided to carry on as usual. Everything, weather included, combined to make' it a great success. Two great incentives helped—the dinner and dance were in the beautiful Village Hall, and the presence of a large number of Mr. Marriott's employees, who built the hall. Mr and Mrs. Marriott accompanied them.

Divine service was held at 12 noon. The members, headed by a new flag, and the Chedworth Silver Band, marched in procession. Again the large congregation can be congratulated on the hearty singing of favourite hymns—it was inspiring.

The Rev. E. C. Hanson, rector of Shipton Oliffe, read the Lesson, and gave an address on " A perfect man."

THE DINNER

At dinner there were 50 more than last year, and everyone seemed to enjoy the good things provided, being assiduously waited upon by the Committee.

As a cricket match was to follow, speech making was limited to a few appropriate words. The toasts were " The King, Queen, and Royal Family," by the Chairman, Rev. Canon EMERIS.

" Colonel and Mrs. Wingfield and family," proposed by Mr. F. ARKELL, who said that he had not been long here, but could find that this toast was really *the* toast of the day. He also thought the village to be almost unique, in that every stick and stone of it belonged to one gentleman.

" Barrington Benefit Society." This was proposed by Canon EMERIS, one of the trustees.

Dr. CHEATLE said he had been treasurer for 31 years, but did not find it at all onerous.

Mr. H. J. BARRETT, secretary, gave a report not only of the year's working, but figures for the 50 years, during which he had been secretary. It was rather astonishing for a village club, namely £22,261 in contributions, £34,216 given to members in dividends and interest, £6,452 paid on withdrawal, £2,107 to deceased members' representatives,

£5,537 to retiring members, and £6,206 sick pay. The number kept up and young men were joining. The Club was in a very healthy condition.

Mr. BARRETT proposed the toast of " Honorary Members and Friends," mentioning Colonel Hurst, Admiral Gilbert, Mr. Marriott, and the Rev. E. C. Hanson.

Colonel HURST said he had been connected with the Club for 50 years. He was very proud to think that such a Club existed in Barrington. It was a great pleasure to him to see the members and Band marching to Church, and he was thankful and grateful to all who had made it a success. May that success continue.

Admiral GILBERT congratulated them on having such a good account from the Secretary. He said : " Secretary for 50 years was good ; 50 not out was better, but 50 not found out was best."

Mr. MARRIOTT said it was a great pleasure to him to see such a model village life. It was a wonderful community and he thanked Colonel Wingfield for entrusting to him the building of that Hall. But, of course, it was his workmen who did it, and they must have the credit. The accident to his foreman was a great loss and he felt it deeply. They were all delighted to come and join in their festivities.

The VICAR proposed " The Committee and the Cook." Their work was most important and it was a great task to carry out the entertaining of the large company.

Mr. ARTHURS, chairman of the Committee, responded. He thanked the company and said the committee would do all they could to make the day a success. He was glad to welcome so many.

OTHER EVENTS.

In Barrington Park a very enjoyable cricket match was played. Mr. Marriott's XI. v. Barrington, the former winning as the home captain allowed the innings to go on after the call of time —a sporting gesture.

Fireworks, postponed from the Coronation, were let off by Messrs. Arkell, Barnes and Colonel Stapylton. A good display and much enjoyed.

To finish the day, a dance took place in the Village Hall, and was immensely popular. Hall's Band provided the music.

Thus ended a red-letter day in the history of the Club, the success of which largely depended on the sterling work of the Committees. The only drawback was the enforced absence of Colonel Wingfield, who was confined to the house by a chill. The Committee responsible were : Messrs. B. R. Arthur, chairman, C. Cambray, W. Hall, F. Herbert, Joseph Sollis, H. Sollis, A. V. Sollis, D. Lobb, J. Tuck, and J. T. Thorn. Others giving great assistance were Messrs. A. W. Barnes and J. Hall.

THE LATE Mr. H. J. BARRETT.

Funeral at Great Barrington.

Widespread Evidence of Regard.

The funeral of Mr. Henry James Barrett, whose death was recorded in our last issue, took place at St. Mary's Church, Great Barrington, last Saturday afternoon, and was the occasion of a widespread manifestation of the high esteem and regard in which Mr. Barrett was held.

The Rev. W. T. Wardle, vicar of Barrington with Taynton, officiated.

The bearers were Messrs. J. Sollis, H. Sollis, A. Sollis, and W. Hall, members of the Committee of the Barrington District Working Men's Benefit Society, of which Mr. Barrett was the founder and honorary secretary.

The family mourners were Mrs. Harvey Curtis and Mrs. T. Lazenby, daughters; Mr. H. Curtis and Mr. T. Lazenby, sons-in-law; Miss Mary Curtis, niece; Miss Hilda Pitts and Mrs. T. Clements, friends.

Among the large congregation at the church were Mrs. Joseph Sollis, Mrs. Hand, Mr. A. Cook, Miss Cole, Miss Pitts, Miss Woods, Mr. C. Long, the Rev. B. Mason, Mr. H. Mason, Miss Herbert, Miss Mulcock, the Misses N. and M. Griffin, Mr. G. Herbert, Mr. R. Messer, Mr. and Mrs. G. Berry, Mr. Papworth, Mr. Mallard, Mr. T. Dadge, Mr. F. Dadge, Mr. J. Scantlebury, Mr. A. Wright, Colonel A. R. Hurst, Lieut.-Colonel and Mrs. M. E. G. R. Wingfield, Miss Mary Wingfield, Mrs. Freeman, Dr. C. T. Cheatle, Mr. A. E. Gibbs, Mr. and Mrs. B. R. Arthurs, Mrs. W. Hall, Mrs. E. M. Clifford, Mr. E. Hayward, Nurse Worcester, Mr. Kendall, Mr. B. Sollis, the Misses Bamford, Mr. and Mrs. F. Arkell, Mr. J. Leach, Mr. and Mrs. W. Bartlett, Mr. and Mrs. R. Tye, Mr. G. Hall, Mrs. Long, Miss Long, Colonel B. H. Chetwynd-Stapylton, Mrs. Tuckwell, Mr. E. Palmer, Mrs. Puffett, Mrs. L. Pratley, Miss D. Mills, Mrs. Roberts, Mrs. Smith, and Mr. C. Stratford.

There was a great wealth of floral tributes from the following: Hilda, Harvey and Mary; Ruby and Tom; Jim and Doreen; Frances, Jack and Geoffrey; Augusta S. Woods and Olive Herbert; Jack and Sybil; the Grover family; Mr. and Mrs. Stocker and Grace; Mr. and Mrs. Bamford and family; Mrs. T. Hunt; Mrs. F. Puffett and family; The Witney Mail Drivers (Messrs. Green, Bishop, Cooper, and Spence); Mr. and Mrs. Lazenby and Peggy; Colonel and Mrs. B. Chetwynd-Stapylton; M. and E. Mallard and family; Mr. and Mrs. Papworth and Pidge; F. E. Greenway; All at Green Drive Farm; Mr. and Mrs. Tufnell and family; Mr. and Mrs. Thomas

Tufnell and family; Mr. and Mrs. Thomas; Mrs. E. Mullett and Mervyn; Cissie Robson; F. and F. Sweet; H. W. Akers and Lulie; Miss Emeris, Miss Frances Emeris, and as from the late Canon W. Emeris; Peggy Fonge; Mrs. Bowell, Louie and Joan; Lieut.-Colonel and Mrs. M. E. G. R. Wingfield and their family; Hilda and Vera; 1st Barrington Girl Guides; Pat and Angela Stacks; Annie Chamberlain; Mr. and Mrs. Tuck, Reggie, and Gladys; Lieut.-Colonel and Mrs. A. R. Hurst and family; The Barrington Parochial Church Council; Walter T. Wardle (Vicar); "Old Friends"; L. and D. Houlton; Mr. and Mrs. A. E. Gibbs; The old scholars of the Great Barrington Church of England School, 1881-1925; Mr. and Mrs. J. G. Leach and family; Mrs. R. E. Benson and Major J. R. E. Benson; The Great Barrington Cricket Club; The President, Committee of Management, Secretary, and Staff of the Counties Society for National Insurances, Oxford; The Barrington Women's Working Party; The Sunday School; The Barrington and District Working Men's Benefit Society; Barrington Church Choir; G.& N.S.; Anon.

The bellringers rang a muffled peal in the evening.

A TRIBUTE.

One who knew Mr. Barrett exceedingly well writes as follows:

Mr. Barrett came to Great Barrington in the year 1881 as schoolmaster. He held that post till he retired 42 years later much to the regret of all. He had a real love for children and they for him. As well as the day school he had the Sunday school, and he continued to take the latter up to the end of his life.

To mention all his activities would be practically impossible. There was nothing done for the welfare of the village that Mr. Barrett had not had a part in at some time or other. He was organist and choir master ever since he came to Barrington, and took the keenest interest in all Church matters. He was secretary of the Parochial Church Council and the Free Will Offering. He was for many years Postmaster, and had at different times run the Reading Room, Cricket Club, Football and numerous other things, but his chief work, and the one dearest to his heart, was the Barrington Working Men's Benefit Club. He was largely instrumental in its beginning and he was secretary ever since the Club started in 1887, and a truly remarkable achievement Whit-Monday, or "Club Day" as it was always called in Barrington, was truly his day, as he was so much the centre of everything. What a contrast it seems that it should have been Whit-Monday that he was taken ill while taking part in an entertainment in the village! He truly died in harness, his mind as young and full of life, and his body as active as ever.

To all who knew him his passing will be a real sorrow, everyone loved and respected him. The children especially will have lost a friend—there was always a little packet of sweets when Mr. Barrett was about.

While the present generation only remember his readiness at all times to come and umpire at a match in his spare time, the older ones will remember how valuable his services were in the cricket field, either in knocking up a score in time of need or in taking wickets. A veritable handy-man in every way.

We can only feel thankful that he did not have to suffer a long illness, which would have been so very irksome to him, but we mourn the loss of one who cannot be replaced, and who was always cheerful and willing and who enjoyed a bit of humour, and our hearts go out in sympathy to his two daughters and his grandchildren in their sorrow.

AN APPRECIATION.

By the Rev. B. W. Mason.

On Wednesday in last week there came to its earthly end the long life of one, who can well be described as a Christian gentleman, and who lived for his village and its welfare. This was Mr. Henry James Barrett, who died at the age of 79 years, and who had lived an active and unselfish life, working to within less than two days of his death.

He was officially the school master of Great Barrington, but he was very much more than this, not only in the sense that he did so much out of school hours, but that to be a schoolmaster was in his sound judgment more than being a teacher. The truth is that he regarded his work as a vocation, a view he always faithfully maintained, and in consequence he believed himself entrusted with the moulding of young lives, future Christian men and women, and he gave everyone to know that he was not just appointed to teach the young for certain stated hours only. So he took a living interest in his hundreds of children, whom he looked upon as his, and was never too busy to help at any time, and to be interested and sympathetic in all their doings.

The atmosphere of the school was splendid, and its standard of work reached to a very high level. Mr. Barrett believed in a sound grounding in the " Three R's," but he especially emphasised also the importance of the all important " Fourth R," which is the Christian Religion. The Scripture lesson began the day, and set the tone for the day. In it the Bible and Prayer Book took their proper place, but the aim was to teach religion, and to train young Christian lives, and not only to impart facts. The discipline of the school was remarkable, maintained by the head master's personality, who also insisted on good manners. School days were indeed happy days; Mr. Barrett loved his boys and girls, and they loved him in return. Besides sound teaching and the usual school routine, there were numerous activities : the children gave annual entertainments, there was a school band (drums and fifes), and the school library bought by the children's efforts, which aimed at producing a taste for good reading.

The head master lived in the village near his school, and simply lived for the village and its people, taking interest in everything, and promoting many things for its welfare. Needless to say the Parish Church of St. Mary the Virgin took the first place in his affection. He came to Great Barrington in 1881, and retired as school master in 1925, but was organist and choir master of the Church from 1881 until Whit-Sunday, 1940. Here again his ability and energy were given wholeheartedly, and he had the full confidence of the members of the choir, including the oldest of the men. The musical parts of the Services were well and capably performed, and the choir was always made aware that its singing was not for its own edification, but that all attended Church to worship God. Mr. Barrett was a regular and faithful communicant, and did his best to set forth the Christian Faith in his life.

Among numerous village activities he was Secretary of the Flower Show, Pig Club, Reading Room and Cricket Club, and played cricket in every sense of the word. He was Postmaster and correspondent to the *Wilts and Gloucestershire Standard*, but perhaps one of the greatest of his works for the village was the founding and running of the Barrington District Working Men's Benefit Society. For the latter Whit Monday was annual dinner and gala day, and on Whit Monday this year he was taken ill when about to M.C. a village social. The esteem in which he was held by everyone can well be illustrated by an incident the writer well remembers. One day over 30 years ago an agitated visitor rushed into the school : a friend was ill and would Mr. Barrett come at once. The doctor and the vicar had been summoned. Why should Mr. Barrett be wanted ? The sceptic might say he could do no good : but he went and his visit relieved the anxiety of all, and the whole affair told of the value placed on him.

On October 17, 1904, his wife died, and although it was a great grief to him, he carried on with everything as usual, an immense proof of his faith and courage.

He served under two Lords of the Manor, Mr. E. R. Wingfield, and Colonel M. E. G. R. Wingfield, and with seven vicars, the Revs. W. L. P. Hand, W. C. Emeris (later Canon), H. T. Dixon (later Archdeacon of Ludlow), H. G. Hensley, W. L. Sloane, G. R. Parkinson, and W. T. Wardle. All worked admirably with him, and the last named laid him to rest with his greatly loved wife on Saturday last in the beautiful surroundings of Great Barrington Churchyard. A large number of people stood by, and they and many others are truly thankful for a good Christian life well and nobly lived. He loved and worshipped God, and did his utmost in the service of his fellows. He loved to quote " Whatsoever thine hand findeth to do, do it with all thy might," and indeed lived up to it. May England produce many such sons, and she need not fear the future

The Late
Mrs. R. Lazenby

FUNERAL AT
GREAT BARRINGTON

The funeral of Mrs. Ruby Lazenby, for many years postmistress at Great Barrington, who died on Thursday last week, took place at Great Barrington Parish Church on Saturday and was attended by many of the residents of the village in which Mrs. Lazenby had lived all her life.

She was the younger daughter of the late Mr. and Mrs. H. J. Barrett, and had been connected with the Post Office at Barington for over 50 years, taking over from her father, as postmistress in 1940.

Her work brought her into contact with very many people and she was looked upon as a friend by all.

Her lovely garden and her paintings of the village gave pleasure to many and her unfailing kindness and untiring work for the parish and for the church will be very much missed.

Mrs. Lazenby is survived by her husband, a son and a daughter.

The service at Great Barrington Church was conducted by Canon Norcock, a former vicar at Barrington, and the committal service was conducted by the present vicar, the Rev. F. Moss. The service included the hymn " Peace ,perfect peace " and the 23rd Psalm, whilst the Nunc Dimittis was chanted as the cortege left the Church. Mrs. Hall was the organist.

Family mourners were: Mr. T. W. Lazenby, husband; Mr. and Mrs. J. E. Lazenby, son and daughter-in-law; Mr. and Mrs. F. E. Hunt, daughter and son-in-law; Mrs. R. Harris, sister-in-law; Mr. and Mrs. M. E. Lazenby, brother-in-law and sister-in-law; Miss S. Lazenby, niece; Mr. H. C. Curtis, brother-in-law; Miss M. Curtis, niece.

Mrs. Curtis, sister, was unable to attend owing to illness, also Mrs. C. D. Clark (cousin).

Also present at the church were Mr. and Mrs. Charles Wingfield, Miss E. Pitts, Miss L. Davis, Mrs. R.Preston, Mr. F. Dadge, Mr. B. R. Arthurs (Churchwardens), Mr. H. B. Parkhouse, Mrs. Hunt, Mrs. Clifford, Mrs. Gibbs the Rev. A. B. Gloyne (Sherborne and Windrush), Mrs. Witchell, and Mrs. Keylock (rep. Barrington Women's Institute), Mrs. Hall, Mrs. T. Herbert, Mrs. K. Herbert. Mr. L. R. Hayward, Mrs. C. Cambray, Mrs. F. Arkell, Mr. W. Arkell (also rep. Mrs. Arkell), Mrs. E. Sollis, Mrs. M. Cambray, Mrs. D. Hayward, Miss E. Sollis, Mrs. P. Leach, Mr. R. Leach, Mr. and Mrs. V. Arkell, Miss E. Arkell, Mrs. G. R. Parkinson.

Mrs. Kavanagh, Mrs. Lewis, Mrs. White, Mrs. Hunt, Mrs. Howling, Mrs. W. Preston, Mrs. D. Mills (rep. Mr. H. Barnes), Mr. W. Preston, Mr. and Miss Bamford, Mrs. Waldron, Mrs. McDonald, Mrs. Ted Hunt, Mrs. Lacey, Mrs. Bowman , Mr. T. Townsend, Miss Dawe, Rev. R. N. Shelton (former vicar at Barrington), and Mrs. Shelton, Miss M. Bennett, Mrs. Norcock.

Mrs. Moss, Mr. and Mrs. Camp, Mr. and Mrs. K. King, Mr. W. S. Tufnell (also rep. Northleach R.D.C. Civil Defence), Miss B. Tufnell (also rep. Mr. and Mrs. H. Tufnell), Mrs. Stocks, Mr. and Mrs. B. A. Bennett, Mrs. J. K. P. Herrin (also rep. Great Barrington C. of E. School), Mr. L. R. Cole, Miss Woods, Mr. and Mrs. W. C. Bartlett, Mrs. Mills, Miss Harris, Miss Kirby, Miss N. Griffin, Miss M. Griffin, Mr. A. Hayward, Mr. J. Hunt, Mrs. J. Hendey (also rep. Mr. Hendey), Mr. C Stratford, and Mr. A. Coombes, Mr. C. F. Spence and Mr. J. Swanson(rep. the Post Office).

Floral tributes were sent by: Tom; Doreen and Frank; Jim and Mavis; Mrs. M. E. R. Wingfield; Mr. and Mrs. Charles Wingfield; Elizabeth, David and John Wingfield; Mr. and Mrs. Lacey and family; Mr. and Mrs. J. Bowman; R. and M. Wood and Allen; Mrs. F. Arkell and family; Peter and Barbara Bennett; The Tufnells, Sherborne; Mr. and Mrs. A. Sollis, Windrush; Mrs. J. Sollis, Elsie and Allen; Gussie; Nell and Sis Bartlett; Hilda, Len, Ethel and Fred.

Mr. and Mrs. D. Hayward; H. W. Barnes and family; Mrs. N. Curtis, Elsie and Dick; Annie Chamberlain and Edith Hartwell; Susan; Witney Drivers, Taynton and Burford Offices; M. and L. Townsend; Miss Holloway and Mr. C. Cambray; Laura Davis; Arthur and Gladys Gibbs; Choir and Organist at Great Barrington Church, Peter, Connie, Robin and Margaret Leach; The Bamford family; Mr. and Mrs. Hendey, Peter and Pat; Hilda Harvey and Mary, T. and E. Stocks and family; All at The Forge, Great Barrington; Mr. and Mrs. K. King; Members of the Prayer Group; Doris, Linda and J. Pitts; Mr. and Mrs. George Young-Husband; Mr. Tuckwell.

Mr. and Mrs. Wakefield, Joyce, Jean and Janet; W. and B. Stocker and Grace; Mrs. Hurst, Miss D. F. Hurst and Col. and Mrs. Mills and family; Will and Gladys; N. and M. Griffin, Rev. and Mrs. F. Moss; Mr. and Mrs. T. Herbert and family; Sybil, Jack and Johnny Meadwell; Children and Staff of Barrington School; Philip Herbert and family; Betty; Ben, Rene and Children; Mavis, Fred and Tony Buck; John and Vera Houter; Jim Farmer, Jack and Joe; Miss Bennett and Miss Dawe; Mrs. Mallard, Edith, Emily, Katie and Ian; Peggy, Ron and Wynifred; E. and E. Hunt, Old Marston; George, Mary and Tony Puffett; Win, Fred and Kathy Groves; Mr. M. Mathews; Barrington Women's Institute; Fred and Nellie Russell, Frances, Jack and Geoffrey; Pat Baden and Michael; Tom and Pat Fitzsimmons; E. Kavanagh and K. N. Lewis ; J. Puschnik and family; Mr. and Mrs. Wilkinson and family.